a Vision book

JOHN NEUMANN

The Children's Bishop

BY ELIZABETH ODELL SHEEHAN

Pierre Toussaint
Father Damien and the Bells
Rose Hawthorne: The Pilgrimage of Nathaniel's Daughter
(all with Arthur Sheehan)

JOHN NEUMANN

The Children's Bishop

by

Elizabeth Odell Sheehan

Illustrated by Harry Barton

Vision Books

Farrar, Straus & Giroux — *New York*

Burns & Oates — *London*

Library of Congress catalog card number 65–11814
First printing, 1965

Vision Books
is a division of
Farrar, Straus & Giroux.
Published simultaneously in Canada
by Ambassador Books, Ltd., Toronto.
Manufactured in the United States of America.

NIHIL OBSTAT:
Very Rev. Msgr. William F. Hogan, S.T.D.
Censor Librorum

IMPRIMATUR:
Rt. Rev. Msgr. James A. Hughes, J.C.D., V.G.
Vicarius Generalis
Newark, New Jersey

The nihil obstat and imprimatur are official declarations that a book or pamphlet is free of doctrinal or moral error. No implication is contained therein that those who have granted the nihil obstat and imprimatur agree with the contents, opinions or statements expressed.

To Agnes Collins

CONTENTS

	"The Children's Bishop"	*xi*
	Author's Note	*xiii*
1	*From the Bohemian Forest*	*1*
2	*A View of the Stars*	*17*
3	*New World Calling*	*28*
4	*"Give Me Holiness"*	*46*
5	*Frontier Priest*	*62*
6	*Son of Alphonsus*	*80*
7	*The Ring and the Cross*	*97*
8	*The Gentle Bishop*	*115*
9	*Through an Ancient Gate*	*129*
10	*The Storm Cloud Breaks*	*145*
11	*The Perfect Disguise*	*160*
	Chronology	*174*

"THE CHILDREN'S BISHOP"

"The Children's Bishop" is the name of a statue that will soon stand before a church in Philadelphia. It will show a kindly figure in bishop's robes. Three children crowd around him, reaching up eagerly. The littlest, a curly-haired girl, already has her piece of candy. The boy is just taking his from one of the Bishop's outstretched hands, while the other hand rests on the head of the taller girl.

The statue is one of many memorials being erected to Blessed John Neumann, Philadelphia's fourth bishop. Others will mark the many churches he built, religious communities he started, his work for education, his wide learning, his brave missionary deeds.

Though no man ever disliked honors more, John Neumann would like to be remembered just as this statue shows him, with children beside him, his pockets stuffed untidily with candy, holy pictures and medals he has brought for them.

Born on Good Friday, consecrated Bishop on Passion Sunday, John Neumann's life shared much more of Our Lord's suffering than of His victory. He was always poor, short of stature, plain of face and often awkward in manner. Forced into high office against his will, he was usually misunderstood, sometimes insulted, always underestimated. His greatest moments somehow never quite came off. It rained on nearly every important day of his life and on many less important days too. There was certainly nothing about him that marks the usual hero.

That was because, except for the children who loved him, hardly anyone knew what he was like. He never said much about himself. It is time now to tell the true story of "The Children's Bishop."

AUTHOR'S NOTE

Among those who aided me in writing this story, I should like to thank especially the Rev. Michael J. Curley, C.SS.R., of Our Lady of Perpetual Help Church, Brooklyn, for graciously making available as source material his authoritative biography of Neumann as well as pictures and other documents.

I also acknowledge with gratitude the help given by Wilhelm Wagner who obtained and translated for me material in German; by the Rev. Francis J. Litz, C.SS.R., of Philadelphia, Vice-Postulator of the Neumann cause, for illustrative material; and by the Rev. William Walsh, S.J., of St. Ignatius Library, New York, who managed to find for me the invaluable life of Neumann by his nephew, John Berger, published in 1884. Thanks also to Mary Farren of Rochester for material concerning that area, and to Herbert B. Reed, Curator of Research for the Staten Island Historical Society.

The Shrine of Blessed John Neumann is at St. Peter's Church, Fifth and Girard Streets, Philadelphia. There too, in the adjoining museum, may be seen a rosary, a breviary, a chalice, an old-fashioned razor and other personal items left by the first American priest and bishop entitled to wear the "broken halo" of the beatified.

ONE

From the Bohemian Forest

"Mother! Mother!"

A rush of bare feet suddenly sounded overhead. Then a small tousle-headed boy ran headlong down the stairs and burst into the warm kitchen.

"Why, Wenzel, what–?"

"Tell him to stop, Mother! He's scaring me. I can't sleep. I–I'm afraid to shut my eyes!" The high-pitched voice faltered as the words rushed out.

"But I thought you were both asleep!" Agnes Neumann exclaimed. Taking her younger son by the hand, she led the way firmly back to the bedroom. By the door was the rumpled cot of little Wenzel. Over by the wall, nearer the window, another boy sat bolt upright staring through the glass at the night sky.

"What's this Wenzel tells me, John? Whatever did you do to frighten the child so much?"

The older boy turned from the window, his big eyes twice as round as usual in the dim light.

"Look, Mother—see the moon there through the window? It's hanging up in the sky all by itself!" He paused, breathless with the startling discovery he had just made. Then he added worriedly, "Doesn't the earth hang in the sky just as the moon does, without anything to hold it up?"

"Of course!" answered his mother in her matter-of-fact way. "Now put these things out of your head for tonight and go to sleep. If you don't, I won't take you to St. James's for the early Mass in the morning. And you won't have the extra piece of cake I saved from tonight's supper either!"

"First tell me, Mother, won't the earth fall down and crush us all—our house, my bed and me too?"

Mrs. Neumann smoothed the thick goose-down cover over her usually quiet son. The winter wind was blowing with a hollow howl outside, and the unheated bedroom was chilly.

"John," she said a bit sternly, "God made the moon, the earth and all of us. He will take care of everything. That's God's work. And your work, just now, is to go to sleep!"

John lay back and closed his eyes obediently. He knew by his mother's tone there was no use asking any more questions tonight. Tomorrow, he told himself, he would speak to Father Schmidt about it after school. Father Schmidt would have the answer, he was sure.

Downstairs, Agnes Neumann worried about John. Wasn't the boy much too serious? Surely such matters should not be bothering the mind of one so young! She shook her head. She would encourage him to learn all he could, for that was clearly his bent. Other than that, she had a simple answer for all life's problems. It consisted of prayer, hard work and charity to her neighbor.

Tomorrow would be Friday, the day she always gave bread, flour and other food to some of the less fortunate townsfolk. She must prepare them tonight, for right after Mass she would take up her well-known post by the door of the house to serve those who might come for help. Tomorrow—yes, tomorrow, she decided, she would have young John by her side to help. There was nothing like giving help to others to take one's mind off one's own problems.

At the kitchen table Philip Neumann had begun to spread out his account books. His face was stern and serious, his straight dark brows making a firm line above his piercing eyes. He sat down, pencil in hand.

"Agnes," he asked after a few moments, "have you ordered the new supply of mineral water from the spa at Marketiny Lazne? I have three new customers for it."

"I'll do it tomorrow, Philip," his wife replied, busily setting out crisp brown loaves of bread and bags of other groceries.

Philip ran his pencil down the neat row of figures on the page before him. "I think we'll be able to buy another cow this year. Business is better than usual."

Although their house stood in a cluster of other homes in the middle of town, the Neumanns, like many families, also owned a strip of meadow land outside the gates where they kept several cows and did a little farming.

Both the farming and the mineral water were sidelines, however. Their real income was earned at home. Philip Neumann had fled from his native Bavaria when Napoleon's army threatened to overrun Germany. Crossing the wooded heights of the Bohemian Forest westward, he had traveled in search of a new place to settle. He had found it in a village named Prachatitz, an ancient town in a rich and beautiful valley. He also found his future wife, Agnes, daughter of a harness-maker of Prachatitz. This land is Czechoslovakia today, but in Philip Neumann's time it still had its original name, Bohemia.

He had chosen Prachatitz for his second home for a very logical reason. Philip Neumann was a stocking-knitter by trade, and in Prachatitz he found there was no stocking-knitter. There he had set up his looms and soon had a thriving business. They were not rich people, the Neumanns, but they were not poor either. Their home was comfortable, and they were able to hire several helpers in the house and at the looms.

"And don't forget to lay out the yarns for tomorrow," he reminded his wife. "The assistants will be here early. I promised to give them the afternoon off in preparation for the holyday."

Mrs. Neumann continued her evening tasks quietly. Silence upstairs told her all the children were asleep.

The whole town of Prachatitz seemed to be sleeping under its red-tiled roofs. Around it in the winter moonlight towered the mountains of the Bohemian Forest, tall and majestic, their age-old pines and spruces blanketed with snow.

The Bohemian Forest is a great strip of trees and mountains right in the center of Europe, running north and south. Curving around the borders of Bohemia, it separated that country from its eastern neighbor, Germany, and from Austria to the south. The history of Bohemia and of much of central Europe was written in and around that remarkable natural barrier.

Through its fragrant evergreen passes army after army had marched as people waged war to gain power over neighboring countries. Many empires and rulers had risen and fallen under its craggy crests, and more still would come.

In its mysterious green depths legends by the hundred had been born. Beautiful princesses locked in towered castles! Witches and evil spirits taking innocent travelers captive! On such wonderful and fearful fairy tales the children of Bohemia grew up, their lives interwoven with the magic of the Böhmerwald, in whose shadows they walked and whose heights towered always above them.

Yet though they might wear a lucky sprig of bramble whenever they ventured into the forest, for protection against the wicked jezeninny who dwelt there, the Bohemian people were deeply religious. They remembered how their first ruler, "good King Wenceslaus," had worked to spread the Christian faith and how he had suffered a cruel death at the hands of his pagan relatives. To be named for St. Wenceslaus was a great honor for any Bohemian boy. Next in importance to the sons of Bohemia was the name John.

Everyone knew the story of the Three Johns of Bohemia, nicknamed John the Goose, John the One-Eyed and John of the Five Stars!

The first was the fourteenth century religious reformer, forerunner of Martin Luther, John Hus, whose birthplace, Husinec, means "goose." The second was his devoted follower, John Ziska, a warrior, blind in one eye, who led the Hussites in bloody religious wars.

The third was John of Nepomuc, known to us as St. John Nepomucene—priest and martyr. As he was thrown to his death in the River Moldau for having offended the Emperor, some saw five mystic stars appear above the waters.

By an odd twist of history, all three Bohemian Johns were especially remembered in Prachatitz. Hus had attended the school there and as a boy had sung in the choir of St. James's Church to pay his tuition. Later on, Ziska and his fiery band laid siege to the town and massacred many townsfolk who had taken refuge in the church. One could still see the cannonballs imbedded deeply in its sturdy stone walls!

Nepomuc, hometown of the saintly John, was only a few miles down the road from Prachatitz. It was for him that the first son and third child of Philip and Agnes Neumann had been named —John Nepomucene Neumann—on the very day of his birth, March 28, 1811, before the altar of that very church, St. James's.

Though stern and strict, seldom smiling and never laughing, Philip Neumann was a good man, just and merciful to all, especially the poor. As Town Councillor, he was responsible for helping his neighbors who were less well off. He had arranged for the citizens of Prachatitz to contribute a small sum regularly with which the needs of the poor were cared for very quietly and efficiently. Whatever was needed—fuel, food, money or work—Neumann could provide, and did. Everyone in town respected and trusted him, and many brought him their problems.

Once he was told that a certain man was regularly stealing small amounts of money from him. He refused to believe the story until he happened to catch the culprit in the act.

"Forgive me," begged the man. "I'm not a thief by choice. I was forced to do it."

"Why didn't you tell me how hard things were for you?" asked Philip Neumann kindly. "I would gladly have given you help. After this, come to me whenever you're in need."

After giving the man some money, Neumann

went out of his way to ask those who knew of the theft never to mention it.

Dishonesty in Philip Neumann's own children was, however, a very different matter!

At one time scalloped dresses were very much in fashion. One of the younger girls, Joan, admired them so much! How she wished to have one for herself! She did the next best thing. She planned a great surprise for her father.

When no one was around, she took his best Sunday suit from the closet and made scallops all around the bottom of the coat. Seeing that they were not coming out very even, she took a needle and thread and tried to improve the result.

The next Sunday Mr. Neumann put on his coat as usual, settled the velvet collar, smoothed the wide lapels and was about to set out for church when someone noticed that he looked peculiar. Scallops on Father's best coat? Who could have done such a thing?

No answer! He changed to another coat and went on to Mass. On his return he had an announcement to make.

"If only I knew who scalloped my coat like that, I would give her a twenty-cent piece!"

Up jumped Joan, her fear forgotten now that a reward was offered.

"I did it, Father," she said proudly.

She received the promised prize, but not without being reminded that she should have told the truth in the first place.

One afternoon the father's stern look softened as he called John aside.

"Look!" He pointed to a brand-new wooden bookshelf, freshly painted and already partly filled with books, in the middle of the room.

"For me, Father? Is that for me?"

"Yes, I had the carpenter make it for you," Philip Neumann said, something closely approaching a twinkle in his generally stern eyes. "You may keep all your books in it, adding new ones as you acquire them. Then they will always be handy when you want to read."

No other member of the Neumann household, nor any of John's friends for that matter, had a bookshelf all his own. It was, in fact, an unusual possession for a boy like him to have at all. Hard-working, frugal and strict, the Neumanns, like their neighbors, did not spend money hastily, much less shower their children with expensive presents!

Never one to express his deeper feelings openly, John hardly knew what to say. His father understood that very well. He was much the same himself. Inwardly he was pleased at his son's enthusiasm for reading. He knew without

John's saying it that his present meant a great deal to the quiet boy.

At school John's best friends were Adalbert Schmidt and Anton Laad. For them, as for all of the young people of Prachatitz, history wasn't just a classroom lesson. It was a living thing all about them. Every time they walked down a street, they saw buildings centuries old, their walls covered with still-bright paintings of battles and heroic deeds. They had only to look up as they passed by to learn of Bohemia's patron saints, her kings and brave men of long ago. Prachatitz, now a slow-paced country town, had once been a bustling trade center where learning flourished, and the outdoor painters had told their stories in inscriptions of many tongues —Hebrew, Greek and Latin as well as their native German. A schoolboy needed no book at all to know Bohemia's colorful past.

"Even though Father Schmidt is our religion teacher," John observed one day, "I think he's a real scientist at heart. I wish I knew half as much as he does. Someday I will," he finished in a determined voice.

"Go ahead. You can be an astronomer if you want to, or a botanist studying plants, but I'm going in for music," Adalbert announced. "I like the songs Father Choirmaster teaches us. Maybe when I grow up I'll be a priest and sing on the altar." Throwing out his chest in imitation of a singer, he shouted a few phrases, loud and clear. Just then a big-wheeled ox-cart came rumbling along, almost hitting him.

"Watch out!" they shouted, and Adalbert ducked just in time. Everybody laughed as a stolid cream-colored ox plodded past, unaware of the commotion he was causing.

Underneath it all, Adalbert had a serious side. John knew that and liked him for it. Most of the boys had their minds only on games and pranks.

"Come on, let's take the shortcut home through the Square," said Anton. "Maybe we'll see some of the fellows catching birds along the path."

"No, not this time," John replied, drawing away. "I think I'll take the regular way. I want to go straight home. I promised Wenzel I'd take him hiking today. Maybe I'll find some more plants for my collection."

Wenzel, short for Wenceslaus, was the youngest of the six Neumann children and the only boy besides John. Maybe that's why they were always such good friends; with four sisters, they had to be! Now that Wenzel was big enough to take long walks, the two brothers spent many hours roaming the fields and hills around the town.

"Come and see this, Wenzel!" John would call out every now and then. Wenzel would obediently come running to see John's latest find, maybe a spike-like spray of yellow broom, an odd-shaped leaf, a frond of lacy fern, or a crimson cluster of cranberries on a low bush.

Wenzel didn't know what the big words meant, but he loved to go tramping with John. Seizing a stray blossom or loose twig, he would rush back holding out his rather crumpled prize.

"Here! Take it home. Put it in your book!"

Carefully holding the offering, John would patiently explain:

"This is called calluna. Plenty of it growing around here, you'll see. It belongs to the heather family. Look, each flower has four sepals, and this pink part is the corolla, also in four parts, and. . . ." But Wenzel was off again, not interested in the lecture.

Sometimes they went into the forest itself, where they walked on a thick springy carpet of gray moss. There grew the tiny bright orange mushrooms, clustered under the pines. There too were delicate ferns in great variety, even the rare golden fern with its armored rootstalk, considered by many to be a sign of good fortune.

Soon John knew each plant by name, and Wenzel learned them too. They could tell which ones preferred the meadows and which grew on the lower slopes of the hills. Higher up the stunted beeches tried bravely for survival, while on the very highest mountains only the hardy pine and spruce could stand, protected from blustery wind and cold by heavy year-round coats of needles.

If they climbed high enough, they could turn and look down at the town below them, its close-packed colorful roofs, the tower of old St. James's, and the massive gate with its figure of a knight in armor, one of the lords of Rozmberk to whom all this country had once belonged. But the hills made deepening shadows over the valley, bringing twilight early, and they would scramble down again to make for home. It would not do to be late for supper. Besides, they were very hungry!

One evening at the table John had happened to make the sign of the cross a little differently than usual. The servant, a faithful old family helper, had not failed to take notice.

"Just look!" she had exclaimed loudly. "See how John blesses himself! He will be a priest some day."

Her prediction was based on old folklore, yet Mrs. Neumann sometimes had a strange feeling it might come true. John was an altar boy now, and so small for his age that his mother could hardly keep her mind on her prayers when he tried to lift the big book during Mass. She was sure he would drop it!

One thing was certain: by the time John was ten he had proved himself a good student. His parents made a big decision. Instead of having him learn the family trade of stocking-knitting, they would give him the opportunity for more education. Perhaps, Mr. Neumann thought, this serious elder son of his might have the makings of a teacher, a lawyer, or, with his interest in science, a doctor. At any rate he was clearly not suited to be a village tradesman, so it was agreed that he should go on to high school in the near-by city of Budweis. John's friends Adalbert and Anton would be going, too. For some time they had been taking special Latin lessons from good Father Schmidt in preparation for it.

One day Mrs. Neumann overheard John and some of his companions talking about their future. Each one told readily what he would like to be—all but John, who said nothing.

"What about you?" asked his mother later on. "What will you do when you are a man?"

John looked away quickly. In the distance, the

granite height of Mt. Boubin, densely covered with evergreens, raised its lofty head.

"I *would* like to be something, Mother, only it would cost a great deal, and I don't think Father would agree."

TWO

A View of the Stars

Budweis! To most people the word means just one thing—beer. A fine hearty brew it was, too, concocted with endless patience and secret know-how from good Bohemian malt! One could see the makings of it in the flat fields of barley, rye and potatoes for miles around. Yes, that was a glass that put cheer into life, restored the tired traveler and gave a man a stout heart for the day's labor. No wonder its name went around the world!

Budweis, though, was much more than a brewery. There was much going on in that busy city on the banks of the Moldau River besides the blending and stirring of hops and grain. To a boy from Prachatitz it was a big metropolis —capital of the province and see of the local bishop. Everything seemed larger there. The Town Square was much more imposing and spacious. Many more stone arches spanned the time-worn cobbled streets. There was more of everything, including people. And most of them, haggling loudly over the price of fat geese and chickens under the bright-colored umbrellas in the market place, were speaking Czech instead of the German usually heard in Prachatitz.

Budweis was indeed a very important city. For hundreds of years it had stood on the main trade route running north and south through central Europe. Along this route, known as the Golden Way, horse-drawn cargoes had passed for centuries, from the Austrian city of Linz to the Bohemian capital of Prague, carrying salt and spices, rich cloth and many other supplies.

That year of 1823, a crisp autumn day, some twenty boys came down that famous Golden Way, walking the fifteen or so miles from Prachatitz to Budweis to enter the Gymnasium or high school conducted by the Piarist Fathers.

One of them was John Neumann, twelve years

old, dressed in a bright yellow jacket, considerably shorter in stature than his fellows, but stocky and strong, his step firm in a pair of sturdy boots as he strode along beside Adalbert.

All Saints Day, November 1st, marked the end of the harvest season and the opening of the new school year. For these boys it was also the beginning of a new kind of life, for most were leaving home for the first time.

At the end of their long walk was the huge, paved Square of Budweis with its massive center fountain. There the group broke up to seek their various rooming houses. John went to the Linzstrasse, where his father had arranged for him to stay with some friends, the Eberles. His trunk, sent on ahead a few days before, was waiting for him.

The Gymnasium itself was not much to look at, a hoary old place that had seen long service as a monastery. Next to it stood the Church of the Sacrifice of the Holy Virgin. If the outside was disappointing, there was another letdown awaiting John within. So well had he prepared for his new studies that he found his classes too easy, even boring. He hardly had to open his books at all, so to use his time well John decided to learn languages by himself. He started with Italian, Czech and French. They came to him easily, but there was another drawback. To save money he had shared a room with several other boys. Now he soon saw this was not a good idea. He made several moves until finally he found a small room to himself, where he could read and study to his heart's content without interruption. There he brought his beloved microscope and books.

Anton and Adalbert came often to visit John, and eventually the three formed a kind of nature club, collecting plant sections and making slides, each one showing the others any unusual specimen he collected.

When John came home to Prachatitz for his vacation in the fall of 1828, at the end of his fifth year, he seemed even quieter than usual. Soon came the moment he had been dreading.

"Let's see your school report, son," Philip Neumann demanded. Shamefaced, John produced the unfortunate paper.

"What does this mean?" his father wanted to know. "These marks are terrible!"

"I know, Father." John did not offer any excuse or try to defend himself.

Neumann rose from his chair, his high-buttoned vest and stiff collar making him look all the more forbidding. "It seems you are not interested in studies after all. Very well, then! It's not too late for you to learn a trade. You're only seventeen. I'll arrange for you to find work. You can start right away."

Perhaps the bad report was not altogether displeasing to Philip Neumann. In his heart every father may hope his son will follow in his own footsteps. The family business would be passed on some day. Besides, thrifty manager that he was, he had no intention of wasting money on useless schooling.

John's mother, as usual, was more understanding.

"Father said I must give up school," he told her dejectedly.

"Now, now," she protested, "you mustn't give up so easily. You've always done well before!"

"Father's right. I'm not getting anywhere."

Many days that autumn John spent journeying on foot through the countryside, visiting the many shrines near by—Our Lady of Gojau, or St. Philip Neri's shrine on Mt. Libin. It was a holy custom among his people to pray at these shrines, and Bohemia was dotted with lovely wayside places of devotion. For John Neumann they seemed to have a special and very deep meaning, especially when he was worried or in doubt. He would return from his lonely pilgrimages worn out physically but greatly strengthened in spirit.

One day Agnes Neumann spoke seriously to her husband.

"Philip, perhaps those bad marks aren't John's fault after all. He never received less than 'Excellent' before."

"Not everyone is cut out for higher learning," was the father's reply.

"But it might be that his teachers don't understand him, or he them. Couldn't you visit the school yourself next time you are in Budweis on business?"

Somewhat reluctantly, Philip Neumann agreed. His wife, it turned out, had been right. A misunderstanding had resulted in an error in the grading of the tests. When it was arranged for John to take them over again, he did his usual good work.

Thus he returned to Budweis to finish his high school course and did so well that he was sent on to the two-year college at the Philosophical Institute there.

Those eight years in Budweis were important ones for John, as they are for everyone. They are the years when minds widen to take in the world; when whole answers must be found and the fragmentary explanations of childhood do not satisfy any longer; when steps must be taken alone, no longer led by reassuring guardians who have been through it all before. It is the time when one looks at life for the first time with one's own eyes, sometimes seeing a very different, very personal view. And it is the time when decisions must be made that will affect a lifetime—many lifetimes perhaps.

What was John Neumann being, or becoming, during those all-important years?

On the surface he did not seem much different from anyone else. A bit more serious certainly, but not too much so. A good student, yes, but that was not very unusual either. If he made high marks, he worked for them; it wasn't sheer genius or inspiration. He was deeply religious, but not in any very striking way. He went to church with the others, received the Sacraments as they did, visited the Blessed Sacrament as they did.

Yet already he possessed the most remarkable trait he would carry through life: the ability to appear completely unremarkable! If that seems to be a riddle, the rest of the story will unravel it. Most of his lifetime, the important facts about the person named John Neumann were to remain carefully hidden. No one knew, for instance, that when he was sixteen, at a time when most young people are eager for pleasure and adventure, he had already quietly chosen another way—self-denial and penance. It never showed. No one saw that while they slept, he prayed. In fact, if those who knew him had been asked what was most outstanding about that young man, they would have answered:

"Nothing."

No one ever noticed him particularly, and of this he was very glad. His appearance helped, for he had stopped growing at not much over five feet. Who would ever notice such a short, quiet, plain person?

He still sat at the window and looked out at the sky on starry nights, only now he knew those distant lights, their names and courses through infinite space. From his early lessons in Prachatitz he had gone on to books of his own—the books of Tycho Brahe and Kepler, of Bode who had named 17,240 stars and nebulae, and of the great Piarist astronomer-priest, Giovanni Inghirami. They had first charted these paths of light, anxious eyes peering heavenward through countless nights in search of new knowledge. They were the heirs of Copernicus and Galileo, pondering the revolutions of the earth/sun or the sun/earth.

He had read them all, pored over them by candlelight till he knew them by heart. For a time his great interest in such things had drawn him into the world of science, a world of facts and figures, where nothing is accepted without visible proof. He had even thought of making science his life work.

Yet behind it all he saw, or actually felt more and more, an overwhelming sense of God. He understood now that the answer his mother had given to his first anxious question about the earth's falling had been the best possible answer. No scientist at all, she had the true wisdom of her simple faith.

Almighty God, Whose wondrous power could bring the Milky Way into being and could direct the courses of those billion-light-yeared creatures, must also have a plan for him. The John Neumann plan was not in any of his books. He sought it through sleepless nights and on long solitary walks.

In boyhood he had looked up at Mt. Boubin towering over the lesser peaks, and had dreamed of becoming a priest. Later he had scanned in much the same way the celestial bodies making earth seem small and insignificant. Just so the vocation of the priest towered over all other possible callings.

But could he, plain John Neumann, hope to attain such a height?

He found it hard always to speak of his feelings to anyone but his mother. She had hoped her elder son would choose the altar. The father, on the other hand, ever practical, rather wished for a doctor or a teacher in the family. He had invested considerable money in the education of John and quite naturally hoped he could rely on him for support when his own working days were done. At least Wenzel had begun to learn the stocking-knitting business.

"Even if I chose to enter the seminary," John explained to his mother, "I don't think I'd have a chance of being accepted."

The diocese of Budweis was then in the unusual position of having too many priests. Every year eighty or ninety young men asked to enter the seminary, but only twenty could actually get in. Those with influential friends to recommend them generally were accepted.

Mrs. Neumann cut through all the lights and shadows flickering in her son's mind. "If you feel God is calling you, then you have no choice. You must apply. Send a letter asking for admission. Whether it is accepted or not, it will be God's choice. Leave it in His hands."

A special messenger carried the momentous letter to Budweis. John prepared for disappointment. He was hardly prepared for the surprise and joy he felt when word came that, against all odds, he had indeed been accepted.

Now he was to begin reaching for the stars in another way. The telescope brought the heavenly bodies closer, but far beyond them shone stars of the spirit no lens could capture. And far beyond the borders of Bohemia, those same stars looked down on the vast reaches of another continent—America.

THREE

New World Calling

"Thrice I was scourged, once I was stoned, thrice I suffered shipwreck. A night and a day I was adrift on the sea; in journeyings often, in perils from floods, in perils from robbers . . . from my own nation. . . ."

The voice of Professor Koerner filled the crowded classroom as he read the stirring words of the day's New Testament text. It was St. Paul's second letter to the Corinthians.

"In perils in the wilderness—"

The phrases of the great missionary-apostle suddenly seemed to fill the drab hall. They resounded in John Neumann's ears as if written just for him.

Professor Koerner was speaking now about the missionary life. Far from a routine lesson, there was something strangely compelling in his voice.

"It may be that Almighty God has chosen some among you here today for that high calling. If so, then you in particular will remember this letter of St. Paul often in years to come."

What is it that now and then touches lifeless words on a page and turns them into living beings? One moment they are merely marks, perhaps familiar marks seen a hundred times over. The next, they are transformed into life itself, calling forth, whether we will it or not, the total response of our hearts. It can't be explained. We only know this particular seminary class struck John with the terrible impact of reality.

His mind worked rapidly, trying to grasp what was happening. Paul wasn't just a name. He was a man, a short man like himself, with failings and weaknesses often admitted. Divine inspiration alone lifted him out of himself!

At that moment John knew he would become a missionary.

Thus do we meet, when least expected, the great turning-points of life.

"In perils in the sea . . ."

Wasn't it foolish for John Neumann in the drowsy afternoon sun of an Old World classroom to see himself suddenly striding heroically across the untamed American wilderness bearing God's Word to countless souls? Of course it was, just as every other great dream man ever had has seemed foolish from the strictly sensible point of view!

"In labor and hardships, in many sleepless nights . . ."

But John wasn't usually given to flights of fancy. His feet in their heavy country boots had always been firmly planted on solid Bohemian ground. How could he be carried away by such a wild idea?

"In hunger and thirst, in fastings often, in cold . . ."

Yet when he stumbled dazedly from that class it was all as clear to him as the doorway through which he passed, or much more so. His future had seized him with an inescapable grip, a grip which would pull him along irresistibly, from which he would never again be free!

The three old friends were still together. Adalbert Schmidt and Anton Laad were also studying for the priesthood. Their paths so far had run side by side. It was not until a few weeks had passed that John discovered he had not been the only one to whom Paul had spoken that afternoon through Professor Koerner.

He and Adalbert were briskly striding down an arcaded street when Adalbert suddenly stopped short and faced John.

"Listen, there's something I have to tell you. I couldn't mention it before, but now I'm sure—absolutely sure."

"What is it?" The look in his friend's eyes told John something very important was coming.

"I'm going to be a missionary priest in America," Adalbert blurted out.

He watched John carefully, anxiously, for the reaction. A startling statement like that would surely shake up even the habitual Neumann calm. Adalbert himself was tense and excited. The past few days had been a turmoil. He couldn't keep his thoughts to himself any longer.

To his great surprise and disappointment, John's expression hardly changed at all. He even joked about the idea, as if he didn't quite believe it. Adalbert was puzzled.

"Look, I mean it! As soon as I'm ordained I'll be leaving. They need priests over there desperately."

John still acted as though he did not take the idea seriously.

Several more days passed and then, as they

stood watching the quiet waters of the Moldau pushing on to the north, John announced:

"I'm coming with you!"

He had known it all along, but he too had found it hard to speak.

Now they began planning together how to achieve their great ambition.

"We mustn't let people know about it yet, Adalbert. It would start them talking, and I don't want my parents worrying about it now. We'll tell them just before we're ready to go."

They solemnly promised to share the secret with no one except their confessor or spiritual director. They still had years of training to finish before ordination.

That day they kept walking for a long time, turning back from the river up into the town, winding back and forth through the cold streets, hardly noticing where they went. It was rare for John to talk so much. They didn't even know how late it was growing until it was completely dark. Their worn jackets were flapping about in a blustery wind.

As they stood in front of the house where John roomed—for the cramped quarters of the seminary could not accommodate the first-year students—Adalbert thrust a book into John's hands, telling him to return it the next day.

That night John pored over the printed sheet

by candlelight. It was a report of the work of the Leopoldine Society, recently formed in Vienna to help send missionaries to America and support them. With the approval of the Emperor Francis I, it bore the name of his daughter, Empress of Brazil.

Here were first-hand accounts of life in the United States of America. For the first time John began to see how hard it was to plant the Faith in a new land. Added to the lack of churches and priests was the fact that Europeans flocking to the new republic spoke many tongues besides English. A missionary had to be a master of languages to make himself understood.

Father Herman Dichtl, Canon of the Budweis Cathedral, was an enthusiastic supporter of the Leopoldine Society. He hoped to encourage young priests to take up the challenge, even though to most European clergymen America meant merely a vast wilderness, savage Indians, privation, suffering and persecution. To be an apostle of Christ in America was almost the same to them as choosing martyrdom!

John and Adalbert read every report Father Dichtl gave them. In one there was a letter from a bishop named Francis Patrick Kenrick in the city of Philadelphia, State of Pennsylvania, begging for German-speaking priests to take care of Catholic immigrants and settlers.

Philadelphia! Sitting at his study desk, John tried to picture that far-off place. He could touch it on his globe, but what it was like he couldn't imagine. That it was not at all like Bohemia he was very sure.

Secretly, yet strenuously, he began to prepare for the future. He knew one basic requirement would be physical stamina. He would make himself indifferent to heat, cold, hunger and thirst. He would learn to do without sleep, to rest on a stiff wooden bench or two chairs drawn together. He spent the night outdoors on cold damp ground and tramped the stiffness out of his bones next morning. He forgot about his dinner, and sometimes breakfast and midday lunch too. He kept his hat on and his jacket buttoned under the scorching summer sun, and refused politely the cool drink he was offered for his parched throat. Some day these things would be required in everyday life. He must begin right away. As his already sturdy body grew hardened through the discomforts he put upon it, his will grew strong too. Constant prayer helped him keep his mind focused on what was now the only important thing in the world. It was all done so quietly, nobody ever noticed.

One important part of the preparation he did not think could be done alone. He must learn as many languages as possible, English above all. He asked the Bishop if he might transfer to the large Seminary of the Clementinum in Prague for his last two years. This was part of the University of Prague where surely he could study several languages at once. He and Anton Laad were the two chosen to go to Prague in 1833 while Adalbert remained behind to finish his course in Budweis.

City of a Thousand Towers! That was Prague—a fantastic tale told all in stone. The first part of the story had been written in Romanesque style, in the solid castles of ancient Czech princes built on the steep heights. Then came some chapters in breathtaking Gothic—the immense yet airy towers of St. Vitus Cathedral crowning the skyline! The Renaissance added its own flowery touches. But the climax of the story was all carved in Baroque, every foot of wall, bridge, roof or parapet embroidered in liquid stone. As the building styles of all past centuries grew up side by side, woven together into a fairyland city, the vast population of stone people had grown also. Countless carved saints and heroes, evil spirits and ordinary folk lived in Prague. They marched across its bridges, peered down from balconies, stood guard over every open square. They dwelt on roofs, filed up and down walls, lined entrance gates. And in general they got along very well with the flesh-and-blood citizens who plied their various trades around and below them.

All this was lost on John Neumann. For him the one-time capital of the Holy Roman Empire would never be romantic or exciting. The mists that often hung over its clustered spires and onion domes signified far more to him. From the huge Clementinum on the heights of the Old City, he could look out upon a thousand years of his own past. But he was interested in the future, and this was clouded with fog.

Disappointment on the heels of disappointment was all he found there.

A new rule had just been passed forbidding seminarians like him to take language courses at the University. That defeated his purpose in coming. He made the best of it, studying French by himself and persuading the professor to let him take the regular exam at the end of the year. He passed it, much to the professor's surprise, without attending a single class. English was not taught anywhere at all, though he did manage to find a factory where there were some English workmen who were glad enough to talk to him on the few occasions he was allowed to visit them.

Most of the seminary professors were sympathetic to the Emperor's view of the Church, which definitely was not John's view. Rules were always strict there, but the recent heavy influence of the imperial court had created a stifling atmosphere. Papal authority was questioned, if not actually denied, and many of the lectures John had to listen to were very much in error. Some of the students and teachers made fun of him when he tried to uphold the correct view. He learned to take their ridicule with outward poise, but it cut very deeply all the same.

It couldn't be denied that John himself had a certain awkwardness about him, a knack for doing or saying just the thing that annoyed some people.

All in all he felt very much alone, homesick for his family and for Budweis where he had many good friends. He had no one to talk to, no one who understood the particular personality that was John Neumann, so he had to be silent. He realized that Dr. Rost, president of the seminary, tried to understand him. John himself wanted to respond, but somehow he could never feel at ease with this man or confide in him. Only his diary records the sufferings of those days.

On Tuesdays, the one afternoon the students were allowed out for two hours, he would walk alone from Old Castle Hill down through narrow streets and steps to the wide Moldau that cut Prague in two, its banks punctuated with rocky spurs and its quiet waters spanned by countless bridges. He would cross the oldest one of all, the Charles Bridge, with its thoughtful stone saints along each curving side. Among them his patron, John of the Five Stars, Nepomucene, gazed patiently at the very waters where he had met his death. He was the saint of bridges.

On the other side John's steps along the patterned black and white pavement would lead him, almost unconsciously, to Wenceslaus Square, the city's business center. There the saintly King, Vaclav as the Czechs called him, patron of his people and his nation, sat in helmet and coat of mail upon his spirited horse, whose hooves seemed to paw the air anxious to get down from the pedestal and take a ride through the city where the King once lived and ruled.

Before the marvelous clock on Old Town Hall, John would shake himself from his thoughts, pause, and look up.

Since before America was discovered, this clock had hung here ticking away history. It was much more than a timepiece. It was a whole play on human life. Every hour the intricate windows flew open and the figures of Christ and his Twelve Apostles filed solemnly past. Surrounding figures went into action too. Vanity stared into her mirror and ugly Avarice clutched his money bag tightly. The skeleton of Death held up his hour glass, grim reminder of time's passing. This clock even told the phases of the moon and the seasons of the year. All man's story was summed up in this one piece of machinery, the work of an inventor who was also a philosopher. John read the story very well.

Now he would have time for a brief visit to St. Vitus Cathedral. Here, beneath awesomely high vaulted ceilings, were the shrines and relics of Wenceslaus and John of Nepomuc. He prayed for courage like theirs. He would never be a spectacular figure—it was already obvious he had none of the makings of such a hero—but he needed the same courage, the same fortitude to meet whatever his future held. Yes, even if it were death!

Through these dark days he never wavered from his resolution. Some delegates had come from the government to offer him a job. There was an opening for a seminarian with a gift for languages in some imperial legation. It guaranteed a good income, a life of ease, steady advancement.

But there was nothing in St. Paul about "perils in government offices." He would stick to the wilderness. No offer of worldly profit or success mattered.

Just before he left Prague, two other sharp blows fell.

Word came that there would be no ordinations that year. The Bishop, over eighty years old, was ill and frail. This meant John must leave for America even without being a priest.

On top of that came another and perhaps the worst setback of all. Adalbert Schmidt, with whom John had shared so long his missionary hopes and whose support had encouraged him through the hard years in Prague, was not going to America, at least not now. John was completely on his own. He had offered himself for the diocese of Philadelphia in reply to Bishop Kenrick's plea, but no answer had come. Was he accepted or not? There was no way of telling. Transatlantic mail was slow and unreliable. Meanwhile, the Bishop of Budweis did not want to give John permission to leave unless a definite assignment overseas was waiting.

Over everything lay, heavy and sad, the dread of leaving home. The time had come to tell the family of his decision. Would anything in America ever be harder than that? He wrote in his diary:

"No fond parents, no devoted brother and sisters, no kind friends will greet my landing on those far-off shores. . . . None but strangers shall I meet. . . ."

One last pilgrimage up to the hillside shrine to pray before Our Lady of Gojau, to plead with her for the courage he needed. Then, back home, he broke the news to his stunned family.

His father, taking it very hard, turned away silently. When he could bring himself to speak about it, he muttered, tight-lipped:

"Then go if you must. But promise me one thing—don't say good-by."

"Father—would you—could you give me your consent in writing? I must have it to show the Bishop." Mr. Neumann complied. It was a heartbreaking effort to give up forever this son in whom he had placed such hopes. The fact that God was calling him away did not lessen the pain of permanent parting for any of them.

Only Father Dichtl still stood behind the plan and urged John to carry it out. Practical problems were mounting. His passport was delayed. He had no money for travel. The Bishop would not give him release papers. From America there was only a puzzling silence.

Faced with overwhelming obstacles, John Neumann made a decision. He would set out for America anyhow, and he would set out right away. Almighty God could bring the venture to whatever conclusion He chose!

Late one night, coming back from church with a friend, he looked up at the starry heavens.

"Whenever you see this cross in the sky, think of me, and I will think of you. Pray for me."

It was as far as he could go toward a proper farewell.

The moon was still shining when he slipped out of bed in the cold room that February morning. It had been a long wakeful night. Now the moment he had awaited with so much hope and dread was here.

Noiselessly dressing in the heaviest and least-worn clothes he had, he stuffed one last small book into his old suitcase. He was ready. It had taken only a few moments, so carefully had he packed and planned this move.

He stole out into the hall, past his parents' bedroom. They must not waken. They must not hear him now. He went by Veronica's room. Only this loyal sister knew what he intended to do. Last night he had called her to his room to tell her. Through her tears, she had agreed to keep the secret.

Now the staircase! He hoped it would not creak. Carefully he placed his foot upon the treads one by one, lest the wood let out a screech of protest and waken everyone.

Downstairs at last, he passed the room where the dark shapes of his father's knitting looms stood. On the kitchen table was his breakfast, set out by his mother the night before.

"I'll be leaving for Budweis early tomorrow," he had told her, keeping his voice even and steady with effort.

Agnes Neumann looked anxiously at her son. She knew what he had suffered these weeks since returning home from Prague. How many trips he had made to those wayside shrines that had always given him such consolation! The strain showed on his face. Everything seemed to be going against him. Her own sadness at losing him was hard to bear.

If she saw anything unusual in his face just then, she said nothing except, "I'll leave bread and milk ready for you then."

Quickly he ate, although it was an effort, stuffing the rest of the bread into his pocket to eat along the way. A cold blast met him as he opened the door. He paused and looked around the familiar room. From this moment he could call it home no more. The thought was painful. He buttoned his coat and went out, bag in hand.

Outside, the waning wintry moonlight fell over the snow-covered roofs and gables of Prachatitz. Silence was everywhere. Even the most industrious townsfolk were not stirring yet. His feet seemed to fall heavily on the frozen street as he went down the winding narrow hill, straight toward St. James's Church. Outside its locked door he stopped, crossed himself and prayed a few minutes. If ever he had needed God's help, it was now. His courage almost failed as the picture of St. James's beautiful altar rose in his mind. Here he had been baptized, confirmed and made his First Communion, served as altar boy, and prayed so many times. The force of the decision he had made struck him sharply on the lonely street. Never again to see any of this!

Shivering, he drew himself up and seized his bag firmly. No time for such thoughts now! Long years of discipline had taught him to overcome his feelings when they stood in his way. He must go on. He passed through the arch of the heavy stone gateway leading out of town.

It was beginning to brighten, and in the pale light he glanced up again at the painting over the gate's entrance. How many times had he seen that same gallant knight in armor, Vilem Rozmberk by name, astride his warlike white charger! How many times had he carelessly read the words beneath:

"We praise old times but we live in our own."

It was the motto of the Rozmberks, ancient lords of Prachatitz, who had once owned and ruled all this country, even the fish in the streams. Today the words rang in his head with a more personal meaning.

He too was leaving old times behind, not merely his own past, but that of his family, his town, his native land, and indeed Europe itself! Determined to "live in his own time," he was being called away to a new world altogether.

He walked staunchly forward along the Golden Way. Despite the long road ahead and the difficulties he knew awaited him, he felt relieved. At least one part of his plan had gone exactly as he had hoped.

From Budweis, he wrote home:

> Dearest Parents:
> By my sudden and unexpected departure, I have tried to lessen the mutual pain of separating from you. . . . The career on which I am about to embark, and which with God's help, I shall faithfully pursue, I am persuaded will bring spiritual blessing on you both. . . .

Thanking them for all they had done for him and asking their blessing, he sealed the letter and sent it off. Adalbert Schmidt rode with him in the stage out of Budweis as far as Einsiedeln, and for once the two friends found nothing at all to say.

It was February 1836. John was twenty-four years old.

FOUR

"Give Me Holiness"

Coming from a land-locked country, he had never seen the ocean. It was not what he expected.

He had found the *Europa*, largest ship out of Le Havre, just anchoring when he finally reached the port city. It had been February when he left Prachatitz and now it was April. It had taken him all that time to travel across Europe. Along the way he had stopped at Linz in Austria, the German cities of Munich and Strasburg, Nancy and Paris in France. The people he had visited were those he hoped would help him to reach America, but for the most part they had disappointed him. The encouragement and financial aid he had been able to find were very little and in some places he had been received with outright rudeness.

Weeks had gone by—time he had not counted on spending—and his little money had dribbled away despite the utmost care. Traveling mishaps plagued him, and his clothes, none too good to begin with, were in sad shape now.

John Neumann looked and felt like anything but a promising missionary as he stood at last with water running in and out of the holes in his old shoes, looking at the sea for the first time through a dismal mist.

He had just enough left to pay for his passage to New York. Bargaining with the gruff captain, he finally bought the ticket for eighty francs, about $120. Seven more francs had to go for the straw pillow and mattress each passenger must bring. By the time he had obtained the necessary provisions, his purse was almost empty. No beds or food were included for steerage passengers!

Captain Drummond, however, was in no hurry to depart. The longer he delayed, the more merchandise he would have stowed in the *Europa's* hold. Since it was the cargo, not the passengers, that brought most profit, the sailing was put off from day to day.

With mounting dismay John counted off the days. If they didn't leave soon, he would have nothing left. As it was, he had to stay in the most miserable lodgings he could find. Plain bread was his dinner, sometimes with a little butter. Someone had stolen his hat. He was chilled to the bone by the raw spring rain that had been falling almost incessantly since his trip started.

Worst of all, in a way, he had lost his little ivory cross. It was in a shop in Paris that he had seen it, priced at seven francs. For him, a great extravagance! Yet he was strangely drawn to it. He knew he should pass it by, but somehow he just had to buy it. It was a very human thing to do. Perhaps owning a beautiful cross made up for some of the hardships and disappointments. Now it was gone.

Finally, at noon on April 20th, the agonizing wait came to an end. Slowly the anchors lifted and the *Europa* moved away from land. As she stood out to sea John Neumann's last bond with the familiar and safe was broken. The known gave way to the unknown world. He was afraid. Yes, afraid of the ocean, afraid of being alone in a strange land, afraid of the future.

In short, he did not resemble a hero setting forth to conquer in Christ's name. He did not feel brave or courageous. He felt tired and sick. His head ached and his throat was sore. His feet were blistered. He was cold, homesick, discouraged. Yet he did not turn back.

He did not turn back, and that was his way —the secret of his whole life. Not boldness, but persistence. Not dashing feats, but faithfulness to what he set out to do. That was why he could write in his diary, as they faced out into the open Atlantic:

"My soul is full of joy."

He had to write it in front of the two hundred and some other passengers jammed onto the middle deck with him. They would have read it right over his shoulder if he hadn't switched to Latin. They could not understand him at all, for they were a rough and ready crowd, about as different from John as they could be. To them the quiet, retiring and religious young man seemed strange. They said it out loud. He was a queer one, all right. He paid little attention to them, even when they made fun of him openly.

Captain Drummond and his big sturdy three-master had ridden out many a storm in their time, with flapping rigging bare of sail, the course abandoned, and the drift anchors flailing helplessly like corks through heavy seas. Today all passengers were ordered below, and most of them hadn't waited to be told! The storm was a savage one, and mounting hourly. The tipsy deck seemed a very frail island pitching in a world of gray water, gray sky, gray wind.

Sweeping the *Europa's* deck with practiced eye, Captain Drummond caught sight of a lone figure clinging to the stay-ropes in the dipping bow. Could it be that strange silent young fellow, that Bohemian who drew the jeers of all by praying right before their eyes?

"You there—come below!" The Captain's voice betrayed his scorn. Any moment he might be swept overboard, this unworldly traveler. What was he thinking of anyhow, to be out in such weather?

The wind carried away the Captain's command and the lone passenger remained where he was.

"Praying for the storm to go away, probably," muttered Drummond to himself as he turned to go below. If passengers chose not to obey orders, then it was no business of his if he arrived with one less at the end of the voyage! He had more important things to do.

John Neumann had not purposely chosen to ignore the warning. He just had not heard it. He hardly noticed what was going on around him. Even the storm itself had become part of an endless tossing pattern of watery time. Soaked to the skin, heavy-hearted, his last bit of confidence shaken, John was almost convinced the whole thing was a big mistake. Indeed, since the day he had left home, all natural signs had pointed toward a bad end to a foolhardy undertaking.

Now they had been many days on this voyage, crowded together uncomfortably. He had no chance to be alone to gather his thoughts. His slender supply of food, all he could afford to buy before sailing, was almost gone. The water was stale, probably poisonous—what was left of it. His clothes were in tatters. If he did arrive safely in America, despite all this, what would he find? A cold land full of unfriendly strangers. Where would he go? To whom could he appeal for help? He had no official papers of dismissal, a formality necessary for acceptance into a new diocese. He was not even an ordained priest. His letters to American Bishop Kenrick had gone unanswered.

Was it God's plan he had been following then, or merely one of his own? Had it been a wild and willful idea, this crossing the Atlantic to become a missionary? Perhaps . . .

Suddenly he was jerked back to the stormy present. The ship swooped recklessly into a steep valley between two huge waves. John's hand, grasping the rope for safety, lost its grip and he felt himself moved, as by some power outside himself, outside the storm even, to another place some distance away.

Just then there was a loud crack high above, followed by a crash. The mast had snapped, fallen to the deck, and now lay on the very spot where, a moment before, he had been standing. Captain and crew raced to the scene. There they saw the strange young man kneeling in prayer, all danger forgotten.

To him the message was clear. Almighty God must approve of his mission, after all, for with His own Hand He had just now removed him from certain and immediate death. If not, why was he not now lying crushed beneath that mighty severed mast?

Then they came in sight of the icebergs, majestic and terrifying crystal mountains glittering above the water. It was a sign they were off the coast of Newfoundland.

On the evening before Trinity Sunday, May 28th, John managed to stagger up to the deck, weak from an illness that had kept him lying on his mattress for several days. Seaweed floating about the *Europa's* prow warned that land was near. Suddenly the cry went up: Land!

Land! Everyone rushed to see. Through the light fog they strained to make out the shores of New York. Slowly the green coast came into view, closer and closer, till they could spot the reddish tinted houses and gaily painted cottages near the water's edge. Some of the passengers shouted for joy, some wept with relief, and others sang at the top of their voices. All of them stood in the drenching rain till it grew too dark to see anything. The forty days of watery desert were over for John Neumann. In the short space of two years, in 1838, the first steamships would make the ocean crossing in only fourteen days. Then the era of the sailing ships would be ending, and the continents would begin to draw closer together till, in our own time, only hours would separate them.

One more delay remained. The heavy winds coming off the coast were growing stronger, signaling another storm on the way. It was dangerous to try to enter New York harbor in this kind of wind. They must all remain on board till the weather changed. Captain Drummond had another reason for his cruel decision. Several passengers were very ill, and he feared the quarantine officials might make him return to France, cargo and all. This he had no intention of doing. So they stood outside the harbor and waited.

Pacing the *Europa's* deck in sweeping sheets of rain, John Neumann felt he couldn't take any more delays. So many unforeseen difficulties had already interfered with his plans. Now this final ironic touch was too much. To be forced to halt within very sight of his destination!

Again and again he begged the Captain to let him go ashore.

Captain Drummond was used to giving commands and having them obeyed. His answer was a firm no.

John did not give up. Six times he came back with the same request.

"But I *must* go–"

It was getting to be a nuisance. The Captain looked more closely at the shabby young man before him, pale from lack of food and recent illness, obviously down and out, yet with such a burning drive to get on with his business, whatever it might be. The Captain paused for a moment. Then he ordered John put off in a small boat the next morning and rowed to the nearest shore.

There was no Statue of Liberty in New York harbor then to bring tears of joy to the tired eyes of travelers. No skyscrapers traced their breathtaking outlines against the sky. But the Staten Island ferry was running on schedule, just as it does today. The famous nickel ride cost about twelve cents in those days!

At the Quarantine Dock on Staten Island Neumann boarded the sidewheeler *Hercules*, the very latest in steam-run ferry boats, and the pride and joy of its owner, Captain Oliver Vanderbilt. The trip did not take much longer than it does today. It was some time around noon when they drew into the slip at Whitehall Street in lower Manhattan.

John stepped ashore. It was the feast of Corpus Christi, and it was still raining. He had about one dollar, in small French and Austrian coins, in his pocket. Surrounded by wharfside hustle and bustle, he stood on the rough cobbled street, in the city of New York, in the United States of America!

Outwardly he was just one of the 60,000 poorly dressed European immigrants to step ashore at the Port of New York during that year of 1836. The city then was an ambitious young metropolis stretching all the way up to 25th Street.

He made his way to Broadway in search of a Catholic church. The brightly colored awnings over the neat brick store-fronts offered him a bit of hopscotch shelter from the downpour as he hurried along. Past dry goods stores, bakeries, bootmakers, livery stables and jewelers he plodded, occasionally passing the imposing mansions of some of New York's first citizens—gracious homes with high stoops and arched white entrances.

John took little notice of it all. His eyes were high above the street level. He was looking for a cross that would signify the location of a church. He grew more and more puzzled. In Bohemia, one could not go any distance without seeing a cross-topped tower. He scanned one belfry after another, up one street and down the next, past St. Paul's Chapel and Trinity, the Old Dutch Church and the Huguenot *Saint Esprit*. All were locked. He paused before each one, trying to make out their names in unfamiliar words. From the Wesleyan chapel he was surprised to see men coming out with hats on, each one smoking a large cigar.

Yet there was not one cross. All the churches he saw were topped with weathervanes. He did not know that the iron bird whirling in the wind preached its own sermon on the American scene, a reminder of St. Peter's denials of Our Lord "before a cock crows." Somehow he missed St. Peter's, already a landmark as New York's first Catholic church, and certainly marked with a cross.

The right side of Broadway from the Battery to Wall Street was a charred mass of ruins from the Great Fire the year before. Ghostly frames, blackened and broken, stood amid piles of debris —scars from the disaster that would take a long time to heal.

The rainy afternoon drew to a close and he still had not found a Catholic church. Lamp posts began to glow as the gas lights were turned on. John's efforts to ask his way had proved discouraging. It is one thing to study English from a grammar book, and quite another to ask directions on a city street. Tired and disappointed, he put up for the night at a tavern. Fortunately, the Swiss owner could speak German. At last someone understood what he wanted. It was worth the last of his money to sleep in a real bed on solid land and to be told in the morning where to find New York's German-speaking priest.

Father Raffeiner, a native of the Austrian Tyrol, had recently succeeded in finishing a church for German Catholics, St. Nicholas' on Second Street. He was in charge of the spiritual welfare of German-speaking Catholics throughout New York State.

"John Neumann? Why, I know all about you," he said kindly. "Only three weeks ago Bishop Dubois sent a letter accepting your offer to serve in New York diocese. But how could you get here in such a short time?"

"I was already on the high seas bound for New York, Father. I decided to come without a letter." John's relief was evident in his drawn face.

Near St. Patrick's Cathedral on Mulberry Street, the Bishop of New York sat at his desk and studied the papers before him.

John Dubois was an old man. His strength was failing. He was a tough and brave warrior who had fought many battles for the Church in the New World and whose courage had never failed him in a crisis. His diocese took in the whole state of New York as well as half of New Jersey. In all that territory he had found only eighteen priests and twelve churches. He had never been a man to dodge an unpleasant situation, but the one that faced him now was not easy to meet.

Many people from German-speaking lands lived in his diocese. Day by day hundreds more were arriving. They were largely Catholic, but they were in danger of losing their faith in America because they could not understand the English language used in the churches. Of course he had Father Raffeiner and Father Schneller, both fine hard-working men, but they had their hands more than full with the Germans right in New York City and Brooklyn. What would become of the thousands of others who had made their way upstate to start homesteads and little farms in the wilderness? Where, on this clear June day, was he, John Dubois, to find a priest to speak to them in their own tongue?

A knock at the door broke into his thoughts. The Negro butler ushered in two guests. One was Father Raffeiner. The other was an unknown young man who looked as if he needed a new suit of clothes more than anything else. Perhaps that was why he had come.

Father Raffeiner's introduction was abrupt.

"I've brought you a missionary, John Neumann, from Bohemia—"

The old prelate started up in surprise. In his confusion he started to speak in Latin, then in French, then in English.

"Neumann! But it couldn't be! Only three weeks since my letter went and—"

"I came anyway, Bishop Dubois," John explained. "I want to work in the American missions. I hoped you would accept me."

In answer the old man came forward and with deep feeling embraced the newcomer. In that wonderful moment all the doubt, indecision, and hardships of the past months—years even—melted away. For John had arrived at last! He was wanted! He was accepted!

Bishop Dubois stepped back and spoke firmly: "I must ordain you right away. I need you! My people need you! How soon can you be ready? I will call you in a few days."

Thus the answer had come after all, for both of them.

The Bishop, reflecting on the matter after his unexpected visitor had left, was sharply reminded of another young cleric of years gone by who had arrived in America in somewhat the same condition. This one had been born in Paris instead of Bohemia, had been a schoolmate of Robespierre. When the Revolution came, this other young man had made a daring escape from France, his identity cleverly disguised and his future in America somewhat assured by a letter he carried, hidden carefully, from the great Marquis de Lafayette to James Monroe, later to be President of the United States.

That other was John Dubois. He still spoke English with an accent, though Patrick Henry had been his teacher, and remembered what it was to arrive alone on foreign shores. Neither in those bygone years nor now had he ever seriously doubted Divine Providence!

Back at St. Nicholas' kind Father Raffeiner put John to work at once preparing thirty children for their First Holy Communion. From the start he loved teaching catechism. It was easy to see that he had a way with his small pupils. The time sped by, joyfully and prayerfully, until June 25th, the great day of his ordination.

In St. Patrick's Cathedral Bishop Dubois, feeble but dauntless, placed his hands upon the young man kneeling before him with authority and solemn happiness. There was not one face in the congregation familiar to John. No father or mother, no brothers or sisters with whom to share this long-hoped-for hour.

At his First Mass at St. Nicholas' the next day there was a crowd, for a First Mass was a rare occurrence in America then. One by one the children of his catechism class, their faces scrubbed and their Sunday-best clothes stiff and neat, came up and knelt before him. From his hand they received their First Communion. Afterward there was a reception. The grateful parents all brought him some little gift as a token of their good will.

Strangers? Yes, but in another way, no. "His people" now were not those he had left behind, but those who knelt at the altar rails of any church in America.

Father Neumann had now but one great wish. He wrote it in his diary on Ordination Day:

"I will pray to You that You may *give to me holiness*, and to all the living and the dead, pardon, that some day we may all be together with You, our dearest God."

FIVE

Frontier Priest

"Two days out from Syracuse
The vessel struck a shoal
And we like to all been foundered
On a chunk o' Lackawanna coal.

"We hollered to the captain,
On the towpath, treadin' dirt,
He jumped on board and stopped the leak
With his old red flannel shirt. . . ."

The opening of the Erie Canal in 1825 gave many rollicking rough songs like this to American folklore. More important, the canal gave to upstate New York a tremendous surge of progress and prosperity.

It had taken eight years, the iron will of New York Governor DeWitt Clinton, and the back-breaking labor of several thousand husky Irishmen to dig "Clinton's ditch" from Albany to Buffalo—425 miles! When it was done at last and the *Seneca Chief* floated proudly all the way from Buffalo to New York, via the canal and the Hudson River, a new era in upstate history began.

The new trade route opened great business possibilities. Now farmers could trundle their grain, beef, flax, fur or lumber down to the nearest canal landing all across the state and put it aboard a barge for distant big-city markets. Sleepy little towns along the Erie route suddenly sprang to bustling life. The call of the packet bugle, the jingling of bells that signaled the exciting arrival of the "canawler" also signaled rapid change for the whole countryside.

As for the barge captain, he was not very highly regarded by regular "blue water" sailors. How could navigating along a four-foot-deep ditch compare with sailing the bottomless ocean? This captain had little to do but sit on deck puffing away at his pipe, while his wife was in the galley cooking a hearty meal and the voice of the steersman was heard every now and then booming out:

"Low bridge!"

Everyone ducked to avoid being swept overboard into the muddy water. That was about the only excitement the trip offered.

At first the barges carried only freight, but soon it became quite fashionable to go along for the ride. The plain packet boats took on a few airs to please high-class passengers, especially the parasol-carrying ladies in their demure poke bonnets and daintily colored cotton gowns with huge skirts.

The barges were pulled along by teams of horses or mules walking the towpath that ran beside the canal. A boy of twelve or fourteen could make a good living—$8 a month plus his meals—driving the team. Nine or ten miles every six hours was about the speed limit!

The passengers sat comfortably on deck as they drifted peacefully around gentle bends, between thick borders of trees, past colorful clumps of meadow flowers and flotillas of offended ducks

Beyond lay the real pioneer country, forests not yet touched by the axe, prowling timber wolves and sleek panthers stalking their prey, huge moose, black bears and gentle deer. Even at high noon the sun could not penetrate the perpetual gloom of these woods, so thick and close together were the trees. There were treacherous swamps, wild hills and valleys tangled with underbrush waiting to be turned into fertile farmland. The canal trip was lovely on a summer day, but the same scene in winter chilled the bones of the hardiest pioneers. Roaring blizzards, mountains of drifted snow, biting cold, months of hard frozen lifeless earth! The woods were trackless except for animal hoofprints, shelterless except for the occasional cabin or tiny settlement. There the Indian still lurked secretly, his burning resentment against the white man's take-over urging him to savage attack on the lone traveler through the forest.

In summer the sun beat down on the open plains with fierce heat and the marshes bred strange fevers for which no cure was known. The only roads were made of big logs thrown down side by side across a dirt path.

Here the missionary dream of young Father Neumann became reality.

"I am in America; I am a priest, a missionary; and I have a flock!"

Jubilantly he had written the news in a letter home. Now everything was happening very fast. Only three days after his ordination he was on his way to report for duty on the Niagara frontier.

Father Raffeiner had kindly seen to it that the new priest had a good suit of clothes, and shoes as well. Neumann also had a bit of money in his pocket, the gift of Bishop Dubois.

He took the steamboat up through the beautiful Hudson Valley to Albany, where, after an overnight stop, he went by train to Schenectady and there boarded the canal boat *Indiana*. The trip to Rochester took four days.

When the *Indiana* pulled up at the Rochester landing, the cannons were booming and there was a holiday atmosphere—but not in honor of Father Neumann's arrival. They were celebrating the Fourth of July! Neumann made his way to the small clapboard house near St. Patrick's Church where Father Bernard O'Reilly, the only priest in that gristmill settlement by the falls of the Genesee River, gave him a hearty welcome.

It was to Rochester that the farmers of the rich Genesee Valley brought their wheat to be ground into flour. Many Germans were settling there. This is where Neumann preached his first sermon, heard his first confessions and performed his first official baptism. It was an event that stirred him deeply, this first soul garnered for Christ, and he wrote of it solemnly:

"If the child I baptized today dies in the grace of this Sacrament, then my journey to America has been repaid a million times, even though I do nothing for the rest of my life."

He stayed only one week in Rochester. Father Prost, a priest of the Redemptorist Order, had come to take charge of the German congregation. The meeting of the two men was the beginning of a friendship that was very important in John Neumann's life.

His real destination was Buffalo, western terminal of the Erie Canal. In 1836, Buffalo was the frontier. Here "the West" began. Through Buffalo trooped the daring pioneers, whole families moving westward, their wagons loaded with all their hopes and worldly goods. Though growing rapidly, Buffalo itself had then but one paved street, many old elm trees, and one Catholic church—the tiny Lamb of God Chapel.

Father Neumann's parish was not in Buffalo itself, but all the surrounding territory, an area of nine hundred square miles!

From his headquarters at Williamsville, ten miles north of Buffalo, he traveled out in a wide circle to places like North Bush, Cayuga Creek, Eden, Batavia, Lancaster, Transit, Sheldon and the lone log houses that lay between, scattered in small forest clearings. There were four hundred

Catholic families, most of them German and most of them recent settlers.

Much as he had tried to prepare himself for missionary work, Neumann could never have foreseen how things were on the American frontier! Bohemia, after all, was a country old in Christianity, crowded with lovely churches, and with so many priests they didn't even bother to ordain new ones. The shock of those early weeks of his priesthood was very great. He found himself celebrating Mass in places much more suitable for barns than for chapels. His letters give vivid pictures:

> The altar is usually nothing more than a table furnished with a pair of wooden candlesticks, a crucifix, a missal, two tumblers and a plate. From the woods around, frequently from a distance of five to ten miles, flock groups of worshippers . . . some on horseback, some in wagons, all in the costume of their own nation. . . . Truly, my dear friend, did I not know that Jesus Christ was born in a stable and died on a cross, I should doubt the lawfulness of celebrating the Holy Mysteries in such poverty.

His parishioners could not help much, for they were as poor as himself. It was a time of great immigration. War and political troubles in Europe sent many to seek new homes in America. At Buffalo, as at all other United States ports, whole families were stumbling ashore, their few possessions tied up in bundles. Their clothes were different. Their speech was different. They looked like a ragtag mob. Many people shook their heads as they watched them coming down the gangplanks.

It is human not to see very far ahead of us in history, so we cannot blame nineteenth-century Americans too much for not realizing that the immigrants were bringing with them much more than their tattered luggage and pale, peevish, wailing babies. They brought also very precious treasures—age-old cultures, arts and skills of generations of nimble fingers, beautiful music, even the Christmas tree we love so much! They brought, too, their sturdy religious faith which they planted wherever they settled right along with their first crops of potatoes and wheat.

These settlers were bravely hewing farms out of the upstate forests, cutting back little by little the primeval wilderness, cultivating the land. They were no strangers to Father Neumann. He was one of them. He too had a strange accent and a hard time making himself understood. He knew about farming and weaving and forestry from Bohemia. His ways were very different from the might-makes-right ways of the frontier. This is how he said the newcomers began:

> The new settlers, on arriving in the district, choose a spot in the woods upon which, in a few days, there rises a log cabin. Then they clear a certain space all round by felling or burning down the trees, where they plant potatoes and sow oats. In a few years these products give place to wheat. Our Germans all live this way in the woods, about two to twelve miles apart. . . .

To some of the "Yankees" in the neighborhood Neumann was just another unwelcome foreigner. Boys liked to throw stones at him and call him mocking names like "little priest." The very first day he celebrated Mass in the roofless church at Williamsville, some rocks came flying over the wall, one just missing the chalice in his hand.

After seven months he moved to North Bush. He wrote home often, but he always tried to make things sound better than they were so his parents would not be worried about him.

> My furniture consists of four chairs lately purchased with some money I had laid by, two trunks, and a few books. For your consolation, I will tell you that the timber for my future residence has already been cut, and my people are rejoicing in the prospect of supplying me with corn, potatoes, etc. I have never yet suffered from hunger; and as for clothes . . . when one garment grows too shabby for wear, someone or other of my good people provides me with another. . . .

The "future residence" so casually mentioned turned out to be a small frame house with two rooms and a doorway so low anyone taller than himself would have a hard time entering.

As for groceries, many people had hardly enough to feed their own families, so they could spare little to their pastor. Besides, he never asked for anything. He felt he could not impose upon such poverty as theirs. Many times he tramped all day, from Mass to sick-call to next mission station without a meal. Returning late at night, he was too tired to light the fire and cook—if, indeed, he had anything to cook! Bread and milk, perhaps a bit of cheese, were his main foods for months at a time. They had given him land to grow a few vegetables but he had no time for gardening.

As to clothes, it was true that one day as he made his way in a storm through the woods, he met a parishioner who "rejoiced" to help him.

Noticing the priest's shoes, which offered no protection from mud or snow because of their worn condition, the kindhearted man said:

"Father, please come with me. There is a shoemaker near by. Let me order you some new boots."

He persuaded the priest to go with him that very moment. But such happy coincidences did not come often.

By now Father Neumann was a familiar sight around the countryside, short, solid and sturdy-looking, tramping from one town to the next carrying his heavy leather knapsack on his back. Vestments, altar stone, wine, missal, candles, altar—everything needed for the Holy Sacrifice, for sick-calls, for administering the Sacraments—went about with him. Sometimes he lost his way in the snow or sloshing through the swamps after nightfall.

A generous man, hoping to make things a little easier for the priest, gave him a horse. Neumann immediately proved himself the world's worst rider! Not only that, the horse was a particularly contrary animal—obstinate, mean and in every possible way a hindrance rather than a help. This dreadful beast delighted in tossing his inexperienced owner off his back or brushing against a fence in such a way as to knock poor Father Neumann head first to the ground.

To mount the horse, he first had to persuade it over to some stepping-stone or fence. Once, with great effort, he managed to swing himself up on its back, only to find himself facing the tail, rather than the head, of his inconsiderate steed. Off went the horse at a gallop, apparently delighted to have such a chance to make his owner miserable!

Most of the time Neumann and his four-footed companion worked against one another, but the priest eventually became devoted to the poor beast, though usually he could be seen plodding patiently along beside it, rather than sitting on its back. The horse made a queer sort of friend, but Neumann was always loyal to it. When the local blacksmith offered to "break the horse in" with rough treatment, Neumann gently refused.

He had plenty of time to look at the flowers and plants as he roamed the forests. As a boy he had studied botany as a hobby. Now he found a whole new world of nature, including many plants never seen in the old country. His knowledge of plants became very useful. His people, when ill, could not afford doctors. Neumann studied medical books and learned to make simple remedies from herbs to help cure many ailments.

One day as he paused a moment to admire a perfect specimen of a rare flower he had long been seeking, the horse, coming from behind him, looked over his owner's shoulder and saw what looked like a tasty morsel. Out came the big tongue, and before the priest knew what was happening the horse was munching contentedly on the precious flower.

But it was the hardships of the settlers, not his own, that worried Father Neumann. Their lives saddened him.

"Many of our Catholics are in extreme poverty," he wrote in a letter. "They live in miserable shanties, some of which have not even the luxury of a window. As a general thing, chairs and tables are unknown. I have seen the dying stretched out on a bundle of straw or moss. To hear their confessions and prepare them for the Sacraments, I have to seat myself by their side on the ground."

One night he lost his way in a severe thunderstorm. After wandering about for some time, he saw at last a dim light flickering through the tossing branches. Going toward it, he came to a very poor hut. His knock was answered by the voice of a frightened child:

"No, no! Go away! I can't open the door."

Again and again he rapped, and finally the door was opened just a bit. In a corner of the miserable room a man lay very ill—close to death—only a few handfuls of moss between him and the bare ground. The little girl at the door was the only one left of his family, who had all died recently of the same illness.

The unexpected appearance of a priest seemed to give the man, an Irish Catholic, a little courage. Hurriedly Father Neumann took out his bottle of altar wine and poured some down the man's throat. Soon he was able to make his confession and receive the Last Rites. Neumann stayed by his side on the earth floor all night, nursing him as best he could. By morning the crisis had passed. The man recovered and became one of Neumann's most faithful friends.

Other adventures did not turn out so happily. Travelers faced many dangers. There were snakes and wild animals. There were also men, enemies of religion, who did all they could to threaten and discourage the priest. Neumann was once taken prisoner in the woods by a group of masked men who planned to kill him. Just in time, a brave parishioner happened to pass by and saved him.

Another time his feet were so blistered and sore from walking that he could go no farther. He slumped down to rest at the foot of a big tree. Suddenly dark figures began circling around him, drawing closer and closer, with fierce expressions. Surrounded by Indians, Neumann, tired as he was, knew there was nothing to do but try and prepare for immediate death. Then his silent attackers noticed he wore the "black robe" of a priest. Miraculously, their attitude changed. They spread a buffalo skin on the ground, gently placed him on it and carried him quickly to his destination where they left him unharmed.

Returning from a baptism one afternoon, the wagon Neumann was riding in made a sharp lurch at a turn in the road, pitching him out backward. It was a wonder he was not killed on the spot. One arm was seriously injured and caused great pain for a long time, so much that he could not celebrate Mass for several weeks.

Whenever he trudged into a settlement the children always saw him first. They flocked around him to greet him, the smallest ones even looking into his pockets. He always brought them little presents—medals, rosaries, pictures, candy—seemingly an endless supply.

One of the first things he did was to set up little schools. The children spoke a queer mixture of German and English. Their parents were too busy trying to survive to think of hiring schoolmasters. From his worn leather bag Neumann unpacked the books he had carried all the way from Europe. How thankful he was now to have them! How glad he was that he had studied languages so much during seminary days!

He built one-room schoolhouses in the woods, on the edges of swamps. Part of each day he spent teaching. He told stories and gave prizes to all who could answer his questions afterward.

He taught them to sing for church services. Sometimes they would complain they couldn't sing because of sore throats.

"I have just the thing to cure that," he would say, bringing out a piece of rock candy from his pocket. Many sore throats came on mysteriously just at the thought of that candy!

The physical hardships of missionary life were many and severe. The trials of the spirit were even harder to bear. Neumann had to go for many months without confession because there was no other priest near and he could not take the time to travel to Buffalo or Rochester.

He had made up his own rule of life and kept to it faithfully. He prayed constantly. On his solitary journeys he went bareheaded, praying along the way. He kept a stern check on his own spiritual state. Some of the things he worried over seem ridiculous to us now, knowing his poverty, his endless penances.

"I must be on my guard," he wrote. "I fear I am becoming miserly. I take such delight in counting money. . . . To resist the vice of avarice I give half a dollar to the servers at Holy Mass. . . ."

He had made a vow of poverty—certainly an unnecessary protection for a man who often didn't have enough to eat!

Still he often felt himself spiritually abandoned. His burdens were too heavy for one man. At times he grew discouraged. It is hard for us to imagine the awful isolation of those early missionaries who planted the faith in our land. To be a lone priest can be a terrible thing.

Neumann had always stood a little apart from the crowd, yet he loved his family deeply and had many friends from school and seminary days. Now he was absolutely alone. By a strange twist of fortune he never received any letters from home during his four years on the Niagara frontier. They wrote him regularly, but the letters never reached him. He had no news of them at all.

Often he thought he could stand the loneliness no longer. He actually thought of running away. Here are his own words:

> In my faint-heartedness I indulged wild dreams. To escape the terrible responsibility resting upon me, I sometimes thought of abandoning my flock, of fleeing to some distant solitude where I might lead a hidden, penitential life, or hire myself as a laborer in the fields. . . . Dark thoughts constantly assailed me.

In answer to his pleading, his brother Wenzel arrived in 1839 to be his companion and help him by teaching the children. The brothers had always been close, and the coming of Wenzel was a great blessing. The younger man's practical skills made him a valuable assistant, and his faithful presence turned the bleak little house into something more resembling a home. Now when John came back footsore and cold, his clothes caked with mud and sweat, worn out in body and spirit, he found a friendly curl of smoke from his own chimney and a hot meal ready.

With Wenzel there, his burden was lightened, but for John help had come too late. The toll of the Niagara years on the physical and spiritual strength was too great even for one who had boasted of his sturdiness as a "Bohemian mountain boy."

How long ago it seemed now, that day in the classroom at Budweis when the words of St. Paul had pierced his soul! All that the great Apostle had said had come true for John Neumann!

". . . I was stoned; in journeyings often, in perils from floods, in perils from robbers . . . in perils in the wilderness . . . in labor and hardships, in many sleepless nights, in hunger and thirst, in fastings often, in cold. . . ."

SIX

Son of Alphonsus

The Iroquois, Indians of the Five Nations, had called it "Niagara"—"Thundering Water." They had looked with wonder upon those angry whirling rapids no canoe could travel, that great leap of foaming spray into the chasm far below. Then explorers carried the fame of nature's "spectacular" back to Europe. In Bohemia, John Neumann and his family had marveled over a picture of Niagara Falls, never dreaming that one day its awesome roar would sound continually in his ears.

Yet in his little house at North Bush that distant thunder was never silent. He heard it now as he lay on his hard cot and stared up at the rough rafters.

For almost three months, since Easter, he had been lying there, too weak and sick to look after his missions. His deep-set eyes seemed larger than ever, and lines of worry were drawn on his pale face. What if one of his people should become dangerously ill? Who would give the Last Rites? Who would baptize the new babies? Who would —but it was a useless question. No other priest for miles around, yet here he was forced to lie week after week almost helpless. Over and over these worrisome thoughts turned in his mind as he tossed restlessly on the uncomfortable bed.

"What is it, John? Can I do something for you?"

Wenzel rose from the other side of the room where he had been reading, preparing for the class he would teach next day. He went to the fireplace and ladled some steaming liquid from a pot there into a bowl.

"Here, John, let me give you some of this soup. It's not quite so good as the kind we had at home"—he tried to sound light-hearted—"but then, I couldn't find the same things to put into it."

Drawing up a rough stool, he sat down by the bed.

"Thanks, Wenzel. I don't know how I would get along without you. But I'm not hungry."

"Of course not," agreed Wenzel good-naturedly. "When you've been sick, you have no appetite. But take a little of this anyway. It will give you strength."

The homely but kind features of the younger man showed his deep concern. John sipped the spoonful of soup obediently. His mind was far away.

"Wenzel, I've been thinking about something—"

"I know, you're worried about your parishioners. But God has been good. So far not a single emergency has come up since your illness."

"That's not all. It isn't good for a priest to try to work all alone as I've been doing. Oh, I don't mean just the physical hardships—I'm used to those. Soon I'll throw off this fever and be as strong as ever."

"Is it discouragement then?"

"That's part of it. A man needs spiritual support. I told Father Prost how I felt, and do you know what he wrote back to me? 'Woe to him who is alone!' "

Woe to him who is alone! It was a saying of Alphonsus Liguori, founder of the Redemptorist Order of which Father Prost, for some time the pastor at Rochester, was a member. It was through his friendship for this admirable priest that Neumann had come to know and admire the Redemptorists so much.

John hadn't been able to put that phrase out of his mind. Night and day during the long sickness the words sounded like an endless refrain through his feverish thoughts. They seemed to beat upon his brain as that giant waterfall miles away beat upon his ears. Just as insistent was the voice that called him to become a Son of Alphonsus in the Congregation of the Most Holy Redeemer! How wonderful it would be to live in a religious community, to share experiences with other priests, to pray with them, to put oneself under obedience to a wise superior!

There was one question, though.

"If I joined the Redemptorists, what would you do?" He felt responsible for this devoted brother who had come so far to help him. Wenzel's broad face clouded for a moment, then he spoke up firmly:

"Don't worry about me. Maybe I'll follow you right into the Order—as a lay brother."

A wonderful relief flooded John's mind. Almighty God had melted away the one barrier that had stood in the way.

So it was that the Neumann brothers were welcomed into the Redemptorist family.

Alphonsus Liguori, a nobleman by birth, had given up a thriving law career while still in his twenties to become a priest. He had spent many years of his long life preaching to poor shepherds in little mountain villages of the Kingdom of Naples. Here had come to him the vision of a band of men "dedicated to the salvation of the most abandoned souls," the Congregation of the Most Holy Redeemer, founded in 1732. The slogan of Alphonsus was written on the hearts of all his followers: "I have compassion on the multitudes . . . like sheep without shepherds."

Eight years before, in 1832, the first two Redemptorists had landed on American soil from Austria. Sheep without shepherds they had found in plenty. There was a great shortage of priests, especially among the German-speaking settlers. These became the Redemptorists' special care. At Pittsburgh they had managed, not without difficulty, to set up their first permanent American foundation. But hard days lay ahead, before the sons of Alphonsus would have firm roots in American earth.

John Neumann, who had the honor of being the first Redemptorist received and professed in the United States, found the struggling little congregation hardly prepared to receive him. Their church was not even a real church. It was a factory. When the time came for him to put on the long black robe, with its rosary and mission cross, there was no copy of the clothing ceremony on this side of the Atlantic!

There was no novitiate, no novice-master, only a couple of overworked priests who were generally away on mission journeys. He himself was left to manage affairs at home. Fortunately he had known and followed St. Alphonsus' teaching since his student days, and his years as a missionary had prepared him well for his new life. Still, there were moments of doubt, moments of discouragement. Was this the time of peace, prayer and reflection he had looked forward to so much? Hardly! Despite his disappointment he remained, faithful to his own ideal and to that of Liguori.

He went on to serve the Order in several important posts. If that seemed quite natural, because of his unusual spiritual and intellectual gifts, it was also very painful for him. It would have been hard to find another man with less desire for rank and position, less personal ambition than Neumann. His whole manner, like his outward appearance, was unassuming and retiring. But he had promised obedience and he obeyed, though he could not always hide the suffering it caused him. His deepest desire, to remain always unnoticed, was to be denied over and over at ever greater cost to his sensitive spirit.

In Pittsburgh, where iron foundries glowed infernally red and men sweated to lay the foundations for our industrial nation with backbreaking labor, Father Neumann built a church. A new church, a real one this time! It rose stone by stone, paid for with pennies, five pennies a week from each parishioner who could afford it. Many could not!

Each Friday the small treasury would be empty and each Saturday the workmen would come for their pay. What hours of worry for poor Father Neumann! He had borrowed some larger sums from businessmen, but when the time came to pay the loans, there was no money. Some people suspected as much, and said so! One alarmed creditor hurried to the rectory to demand his money right away.

Neumann had not a cent to give him, yet he could not say so. Then the story would quickly spread, causing all who had lent money to ask for it immediately. This would mean financial ruin. He had to think fast.

"Do you want it in gold or silver?" he asked his caller calmly.

"Oh," replied the surprised man, "if you are so well off that you can give me a choice, then keep the money! I trust you completely."

There was hardly time for Neumann, superior at the Pittsburgh house, to do all that must be done. That was because he always took the hardest and least pleasant assignments, the longest trips, the latest sick-calls, the worst weather.

On one of his trips to give a mission, he had to stop overnight at a kind of tavern. Instead of being given a room, he and his companion, Father Seelos, were left sitting in the main hall all night. Taking off his coat, Neumann spread it over the hard bench and told Father Seelos to lie down and rest. He himself spent the uncomfortable hours till dawn sitting up in a straight chair.

But this was not unusual. He might have done so anyway, had he been lodged in the best appointed bedroom in the land. At home in Pittsburgh, where he had to share a room with Father Seelos with only a curtain for partition, he often prayed far into the night, sleeping so little that Father Seelos wondered how he could go on. When the thunder rolled and the skies poured torrents of rain, they often had to flee to chairs downstairs to rest, for the leaky roof soon flooded the room and drenched the beds.

Yet every morning, before anyone else was awake, Neumann would slip down to get a scuttle of coal and light the fires to take the chill off the place before the others rose.

It could not go on like that. Hardship and penance again took their toll. For the second time in his life, Father Neumann became seriously ill. He tried to ignore it, but his racking cough, the bright spots of fever on his cheeks, his all too evident exhaustion worried the others. Finally he had to be ordered to the doctor. The decision was drastic. It was either rest–immediate, long, and total–or certain and early death!

As the first home of Catholicism in America, aristocratic old Baltimore could look down upon other cities. It had to its credit a long line of "firsts" no other place could claim.

In 1632, King James I of England had given the first Lord Baltimore a charter to settle a certain territory lying north of the Potomac River and south of the fortieth parallel on the North American continent. This became the province of Maryland, first and only Catholic colony on these shores.

In 1776, Charles Carroll of Carrollton, a Maryland Catholic, fixed his bold signature upon the Declaration of Independence, and likewise upon the pages of history.

In 1790, John Carroll became first bishop of the first diocese in the United States: Baltimore.

In 1821, the first American cathedral, St. Mary's in Baltimore, was finished, designed by the architect Latrobe who also built the capitol in Washington.

This city that combined sultry southern charm with northern industry had won renown in other ways as well. Its port was one of the best and busiest. Its clippers were famous around the world. There a young lawyer named Key had in 1814 finished, at a tavern table, "The Star-Spangled Banner," inspired by the sight of British troops burning Fort McHenry at night. There too one of America's few genuine literary geniuses, Edgar Allen Poe, had begun writing his weird but fascinating tales, in an attic room shared with his dying brother.

At St. Alphonsus' in Baltimore, the Redemptorists had now established their main American headquarters. Here the unwilling patient, John Neumann, was sent under strict orders to do nothing but recover, if possible, his shattered health.

Hardly had he arrived when word came from Europe that a new General Superior had been appointed to take charge of the ten Redemptorist foundations in the United States. The new Superior, the letter stated, was none other than Neumann. His past work had shown his exceptional ability. He seemed in every way an ideal religious, one who would keep the Rule of St. Alphonsus down to the last letter, and at the same time guide his brothers with loving care. They could not know, in far-off Austria, that their man was at that moment lying close to death.

On that March day in 1847, Neumann saw clearly it was no time to leave this earth. God had more work waiting and, much as he hated important positions, he must get busy. Gathering together his feeble strength, he took his one patched and faded and worn black habit down from its hook, put it on, and resolutely placed the cord of the cross around his neck.

He moved downstairs to the smallest room in the house, the one nearest the front door. There he would be easily found by all who looked for him, whether it was a member of his Order, whose father in religion he now was, or a stranger in need, whose father in spirit every true priest must be.

To this plain little room in the cramped house of St. Alphonsus' on Baltimore's Saratoga Street, many troubled souls found their way. To no one was the door shut. The quiet priest with the unassuming manner and gentle ways was always ready to listen, to encourage, to give, to be bored by tiresome people, even to be insulted.

Above all, he was ready to hear the children. He had written a catechism for them that was to be used for many years, from whose worn and ragged pages many would learn the first truths of faith. It was when he was with them that his great gift showed. He himself had long since crossed the line that separates children from grownups in age, and too often in understanding. Yet he knew what children feel, how they can suffer, how much they need to learn to get on in this world, and how best to help them learn it.

They loved him. He had only to appear on the street to be surrounded promptly by children. They would crowd him as he walked, bumping into him in their eagerness to tell him something, hanging to his hands to gain his attention. They even used to look into his pockets to see if he had any candy for them. Usually he did! Always he had wonderful, funny stories.

One boy had caused so much trouble in school that the Sisters had said they could keep him no longer.

"Bring him to me," Neumann advised the worried father. "I'll teach him for a while every day until he learns to do better."

To the Sisters he was always saying: "Be patient a little longer. Maybe his attitude will change. We shouldn't be too quick to send away those we call trouble-makers. They all have a better side. Let's try to find it."

The children of St. Alphonsus' School could

not have explained it, but in some mysterious way he seemed to be on their side. He often visited the classrooms. He liked to prepare them himself for their First Communion, and he always saw to it that this was a very special day for every one of them.

"Father Neumann looked right into my heart," one of the small girls told her teacher. The children didn't mind that, for he seemed to understand what he saw there even when it was mischief or laziness.

Mother Caroline, of the School Sisters of Notre Dame, knew exactly how it felt. She herself had to admit she sometimes—well, quite often—lost her temper in the classroom and began to scold loudly. She never stopped to think how she sounded till one day when things were going rather badly, she suddenly realized Father Neumann had come in and was standing unnoticed in the room.

"Sister," he said quietly, "I thought I heard you raise your voice just now—"

Mother Caroline never forgot that moment, those few words, that look. They came back to her every time she began to feel short-tempered. They made her pause on the brink of many an impatient word.

At night he never could rest until he knew all

the Fathers and Brothers were safely home. If any were out on sick-calls or mission journeys, he would wait up, making frequent trips to the door to peer anxiously out for the missing member of his family. Twice a year he went over the wardrobe of each one, surprising them by leaving in their cells new clothes to replace the worn-out ones. As for himself, he kept right on patching the same threadbare habit, and, since he was Superior, no one could order him a new one.

The searching glance of Father Neumann's deep-set eyes could, it is true, prove uncomfortable. It can be very unpleasant to feel one's thoughts being read, especially if those thoughts are not very edifying. The priest therefore quite often met hatred and malice in the faces of others, reflected from their hearts. He saw guilt. He saw sin and the fruits of sin. Some called him ugly names on the street, insulting him and all he stood for with curses. Resentment and ill feeling came to the surface before his clear gaze. John Neumann carried with him through life this strange, uncomfortable and even agonizing power.

While taking a boat trip to visit a distant mission, he fell asleep on deck. Some boys stole up behind him and marked his coat all over with chalk crosses. They hid, watching to see some fireworks when he awoke. He disappointed them.

"Oh, that's nothing," he shrugged. "It'll soon rub off." Then he opened the paper sack he carried, and took out a dry biscuit which was to serve as his dinner.

He never looked like an important person and was often taken for other people, or overlooked entirely. Arriving early one morning at the Redemptorist house in New York, he asked to see the Superior, only to be told rather sharply by the young Brother Porter to wait outside. A few minutes later, when the embarrassed porter saw his own Superior come down, kneel before the meek and shabby visitor and ask his blessing, he was covered with shame. How could he know this little man was the Father Provincial of all American Redemptorists? Neumann realized the young Brother's predicament and, calling him later, told him he had done the right thing in not admitting a stranger at that hour of the day, assuring him that no ill feelings were held against him.

Relieved of his position as General Superior by a change in administration within the Order, he stayed on at Saratoga Street as rector of St. Alphonsus', his advice sought on all important matters in the parish and community. Long hours into the night he worked at his bare table, copying the guidebook for novices in his own small neat handwriting, arranging the rules of the Congregation so they could be printed in English, worrying over debts, counseling and consoling all who sought him.

Among those who most valued his help was the tall distinguished-looking Archbishop of Baltimore, Francis Patrick Kenrick. The Irish-born prelate, leading member of the American clergy, had recently taken over the pioneer archdiocese after serving for twenty-one years as Bishop of Philadelphia. Every week he came to confession to Father Neumann, and every week his respect for the Redemptorist spiritual director grew.

How strange that they should meet like this! It had been Kenrick's letters in the Leopoldine Society bulletins that had encouraged the young student of Budweis in his dream of dedicating his life to the American missions. It was to Kenrick that he had written to offer his services on leaving the Prague seminary. That plan, for some mysterious reason, never worked out. Yet the paths of the two men were bound to cross. Now, many years later, in the austere little cell on Saratoga Street, the one-time student was the wise confessor. The noted churchman, whose long-awaited summons had never arrived, was the penitent.

One afternoon as Kenrick was about to leave,

he turned back, a puzzling smile on his handsome good-natured face.

"Oh, Father Neumann," he said lightly, "Philadelphia is without a bishop, you know. Perhaps you'd better see about getting yourself a miter!"

SEVEN

The Ring and the Cross

It was no use—all his pleading with Kenrick, his frantic letters to Rome, the novenas the good nuns made, at his insistence, for the mysterious intention of "removing a terrible danger that threatens one of our large dioceses."

None of it was any use.

On March 19th, the feast of St. Joseph, Archbishop Kenrick appeared unexpectedly at the door of St. Alphonsus'. Having received no answer to his knock on Neumann's door, he went in and found the room empty. Quietly he opened a package he carried and laid the contents on the bare table. Just as quietly, he left.

When Neumann returned, his eye was immediately caught by a brilliant gleam. There on the table lay the ring and the cross Kenrick himself had worn as Bishop of Philadelphia. Like a stroke of doom their meaning fell upon the unhappy priest. There could be no denying this wordless message. No longer was there any hope that he could escape the position whose responsibilities he dreaded. Shaken as never before, he fell to his knees and passed the whole night in prayer.

Next morning Archbishop Kenrick brought the official papers that made John Nepomucene Neumann the fourth Bishop of Philadelphia. The Holy Father had taken an unusual step. Knowing very well the reluctance of the humble Redemptorist to assume high office, the Pope commanded Neumann under obedience to accept the post.

Ordered by his religious superior to write the story of his life on this occasion, Neumann managed with difficulty to cover four small pages. He ended with these words:

> Tomorrow, March 28th, my birthday, which this year falls on Passion Sunday, I shall, if nothing prevents, be consecrated Bishop in St. Alphonsus' Church, by Mst. Rev. Archbishop Kenrick. But do thou, O Lord, have mercy on us! Jesus and Mary, pity me! Passion of Christ, strengthen me!

Asked by another priest how he felt on the eve of that great event, he replied:

"I would rather die tomorrow than be consecrated a bishop!"

After the long colorful ceremonies of consecration, the new bishop went into the recreation room where his fellow Redemptorists waited to offer their congratulations and ask his blessing. They gathered around, admiring his brilliant new robes, gifts of the German Catholics of Baltimore.

"You see," he told them with a smile, "the Church treats her bishops as a mother treats a little child. When she wants to give him something hard to do, she first gives him new clothes!"

Two days later he stepped off the train in Philadelphia. The forty-one-year-old priest who had never wanted to be anything more than a poor missionary had come to take possession of a huge diocese of 35,000 square miles, including the eastern half of Pennsylvania, all of Delaware, and southern New Jersey.

As usual, it was pouring rain. Only a few damp stragglers were on hand when the small figure stepped down on the platform. A little group of priests came forward to welcome their new shepherd. Like most of the truly great moments in John Neumann's life, this one did not quite come off. It was bleak, lonely, limping. Perhaps it was just as well no bands were playing, no banners flying, no paraders waiting to escort him triumphantly to his new home. They would not have been in character—in Neumann's character, that is.

Philadelphia was then the third largest city in the United States. A nation had been born there. The deep-toned bell in the Old State House Tower had proclaimed the Declaration of Independence. In Independence Hall the Federal Constitution had been written. There stood the house of William Penn and the printing press of Benjamin Franklin. Washington served in Philadelphia his term of office as President of the United States.

In 1852 Philadelphia was much more than the "Cradle of Liberty." As "big" American cities went, it claimed preeminence in tradition and social prominence. A center of culture, it prided itself on its many learned and artistic societies and institutions. Behind the stately brick houses with their scrubbed white marble steps lived many wealthy and famous families, prosperous descendants of Pennsylvania's first Quaker settlers.

On the other hand, the city was beginning to take the lead industrially. Though one hundred miles away from the Atlantic, its position on the Delaware and Schuylkill Rivers made it accessible to ocean steamers. Through its busy port streamed countless European immigrants seeking religious or political freedom. Many of these were Catholics from German-speaking countries.

When John Neumann moved into the bishop's house on Logan Square he took charge of much more than a few churches, schools and rectories. Never for a moment did the dignity of his position cloud his vision of what he had actually claimed—the souls of all who lived within his diocese, each one of infinite value, each one worth his supreme effort!

The stark gloomy halls of the county jail were part of it. The keys of the warden clanked hollowly, and he shook his head in a rough gesture to the small man who walked briskly beside him.

"It's useless, I tell you," he repeated. "They won't listen. Hardened criminals they are, tough as they come! They're going to insult you. . . ."

"I'm prepared for that," replied the short man. "I'll try anyway."

One last heavy door swung behind them. They had come to the cell of the condemned—the two Skrupinski brothers doomed to die on the gallows for murder. The prisoners glanced up with sullen faces and dull eyes at the sound of footsteps.

"Look—a priest!" muttered one bitterly. "Go away! We don't want any priests here!" He spat savagely through the bars at the visitor outside.

"Good luck!" said the warden, moving off. "I'll wait for you outside. Signal when you've had enough."

John Neumann faced the two desperate men. Everyone knew about them. The sensational case had been the talk of Philadelphia for weeks. The Bishop in his first few days there had heard the gruesome story. He also heard that the criminals were Catholic. He had come, against all sensible advice, because their souls, he knew, were in his charge.

Quietly he began talking to them, overlooking their insults. After some time they began to hear what he was saying. In the shadow of the gallows, in the shadow of death, they listened to a stranger's low voice. His words began to take effect. Soon the Skrupinski brothers would be cast violently from the world of men, but the world of God, they now heard, had not yet cast them out. Something like eternal hope flickered before their hardened gaze as the little man spoke. He talked to them like a father, not a judge. Like a father, he spoke of forgiveness.

Finally one spoke.

"All right then, send the priest if you want to. We're ready." He had not thought of God in a long time. God, he saw now, had not been so forgetful. The little man turned and left. The priest came the next day, and for many days and weeks after that. The brothers died on schedule—and in peace.

At his consecration Neumann had been asked, according to ancient custom:

"Will you teach the people?"

His answer, "I will," had been no mere formality.

On his arrival in Philadelphia a welcome-gift had been waiting. A new school was to be built in his honor. Nothing could have pleased him more. Nothing could have symbolized better what came to be considered his greatest work.

Very soon he called a meeting to talk about Catholic schools. He set up a Central Board of Education to direct all the schools, for until then each one had been run by whatever pastor or parish had built it. From Neumann's plan grew our present parochial school system. He is credited with being its founder. It was all part of a dream he had—to see every Catholic child given the chance to attend a school where religious values would be most important. This dream and its fulfillment was to occupy much of his time for the rest of his life, and to tell all that he accomplished would take a book in itself.

Of course the children of Philadelphia in those days did not know they and their bishop were making history. They only knew they had a wonderful friend not much bigger than themselves who visited them often and never came empty-handed.

His pockets were treasure-troves to be closely examined. There were pretty colored holy pictures, medals and rosaries, little souvenirs, generous-sized pieces of hard candy! Some would be given as prizes for the right answers to the catechism quiz. Others would be—just given!

In his shabby bag the Bishop often brought a marvelous thing called a microscope. He would put a drop of ordinary water under the glass lens and turn the dials carefully for correct focus. Then everyone had a turn to squint through the eyepiece at a surprising new world. The drop of water had apparently come alive. Each small squiggle and spot the Bishop would point out and explain, just as the good Father Schmidt had done for him when he was a boy at the school in Prachatitz. Teachers and parents sometimes felt they ought to cut short these sessions. After all, the Bishop was a very important man, a very busy one, and the children asked so many tiresome questions!

But something in the Bishop's face stopped them from interfering too much. Anyone could see he was enjoying himself. With grownups he was usually very reserved. Some even thought him unfriendly. He had no talent for making conversation, and he often thought it a waste of time, but all his aloofness disappeared the moment young people gathered around him. He would tell them as many stories as they wanted to hear, mixing up the funny ones with the serious ones and answering all their questions without a trace of impatience.

He wasn't a bit hard to talk to, the children found. His plain features were not what they noticed. They saw only the kindly eyes, the sincere smile of a friend.

Sitting in an office behind closed doors, wearing rich robes and being an important church official did not appeal to Neumann at all. He did as little of that as possible, thereby offending some who liked pomp and show. He would much rather be out making the rounds of some school, hospital or orphanage, handing out books and games, seemingly with all the time in the world to pause at each desk or bedside and hear each one's story, with one of his own to tell in reply.

Stopping at St. Vincent's Convent one day, he found the nuns trying to solve a problem. One of their smallest children had to be taken from there to another orphanage some distance away. There was no one to make the journey with her.

"Let me take her," Neumann said.

"But she is very small and frail. In fact, she is sick. I'm afraid it would be very troublesome for you."

"Not at all. Get her ready and we'll go."

The child was indeed in a sad condition. Frightened and ill, she hesitantly set off, her small hand held firmly by Bishop Neumann. On the trip she became worse. He carried her. She slept fitfully as he held her, and whenever she opened her eyes he was there, talking softly, trying to make her more comfortable. When they reached their destination she did not want to part with her gentle guardian. He had looked after her every moment of the way—father, mother, nurse, doctor all combined. She had no family of her own.

She never forgot that trip. Ever after she thought of the Bishop as a special kind of father, as close to one as she had known. She would point him out proudly as "*my* priest."

Many children remembered things like that.

The altar boys at St. John's remembered. Weeks before Easter the Bishop had made them a special promise.

"On the feast of the Resurrection I'll have a gift for each one of you."

After the Easter Mass, he called them all into the sacristy. Untying a large, brightly colored bandana kerchief, he drew out a gaily colored egg for each. He had carried them himself that morning from the bishop's residence in Logan Square, taking care that not one would be cracked or broken.

One place he visited often was Eden Hall, the college for girls run by the Madames of the Sacred Heart. The first day he brought little gifts for all the girls, met their parents, and encouraged their teachers who were undergoing rather hard times just then. He returned often, always on "special days."

Once the botany class was puzzling over a certain flower. They had looked it up in all their books, and its name was not to be found anywhere. Just then a visitor appeared in the classroom doorway.

"Oh, Bishop Neumann, perhaps you could help us—"

He studied the mysterious flower for a moment or two, then quickly named it. "And if you want to know more about it," he added, "I'll tell you where to look."

It is said he had memorized the names of over

five hundred flowers before his own college days!

Another time it was a problem in astronomy. "Our textbook must be wrong," one of the girls finally announced. "Here's what it says . . . but it can't be right. . . ."

The Bishop laughed at the predicament. "Maybe I can make things a bit clearer. Now you see this star here–"

In simple language he went on to solve the difficulty, upholding the authority of the textbook writer and at the same time careful to leave all the heavenly bodies in their proper places in the sky.

Yet others who talked to him never suspected how learned he was, for his words were always simple and easy to understand.

From that time on there were three sides to John Neumann's life. One was the official side: churches and schools to be built and staffed, money to be raised, confirmations to be administered, ceremonies to be attended, sermons to be given and pastoral letters published, the spiritual and business affairs of the diocese to be managed. Also on the official side, there was the First Plenary Council in Baltimore to attend in 1852, an important event for the American Church, bringing together for the first time all the bishops and archbishops of the country. Most of them, like Neumann, were foreign-born. He was given the job of writing a new large German catechism.

Then there was the unofficial life. Here were a multitude of things not strictly the duties of a bishop, yet very essential to the proper functioning of the diocese. The nuns and priests serving under Bishop Neumann soon realized they did not have to bear their trials alone. Neumann's own desolate years in upstate New York had taught him the need of encouragement for those pioneer foundations.

He once came into a convent where the nuns were almost destitute. One of the Sisters admitted under his questioning that it wasn't easy for them to get along.

"Sometimes we have nothing to make a fire with," she confessed, "and then, when we have the fire, we have nothing to cook."

Neumann looked up at the crucifix, the only object on the room's bare walls.

"Study that book, Sisters. It will make your own cross lighter."

His way of speaking had a strange effect on them all. Something in his words gave them new courage and hope. The shabby room suddenly appeared almost beautiful.

It was one of the few times when the third side of Neumann's life could be glimpsed. Most of the time this part was well hidden. His own spiritual life, the lessons he himself had read from that crucifix, were never revealed by him.

Afterward, knowing that the poor nuns needed something substantial—a good dinner perhaps—to sustain them, he gave them fifty dollars in gold.

He was always giving away money, slipping it so quietly into the hands of the poor that no one else ever knew. If his pockets were empty, which they often were, he would manage to give something else—clothes, food, whatever he could find. It soon became known that anything given to Bishop Neumann would quickly be passed into other hands.

Sometimes this turned out to be quite funny. One day when he was at home two little girls came, bringing him a message from the Holy Cross Sisters. During their visit they seemed to be fascinated by a statue in the Bishop's parlor: a marble figure of a child in a cradle.

Suddenly the Bishop said, "I'll give that statue to whichever one of you can carry it home."

He knew, of course, that neither one could ever budge thirty pounds of marble, not to mention carrying it all the way home. But one of the girls, Margaret McSheffery, ran home and brought back her little wagon. The joke was on the Bishop after all!

"You've won it fairly," he told her, "and you may have it."

When the nuns heard about it they were very displeased and ordered Margaret to return the statue, but the Bishop wouldn't have it. He wished her to keep it. Many years later, Margaret became Mother General of the Holy Cross Sisters and her prized statue is still treasured at their motherhouse!

Sometimes people scolded the Bishop for being too generous. Not all the poor who begged help were so deserving, they warned him. Why, some were just taking advantage of him, coming back two or three times, or using the money for jaunts on the newly opened Philadelphia trolley line instead of buying food! Such tales did not disturb the Bishop at all.

"I gave the money to God," he would answer, and drop the subject there.

Everyone knew that the time to come for help was when they were sure the Bishop was home. No one else would be so generous!

One day a woman asked for a dollar and he had none to give her. Just then someone else came in and gave him a Mass offering of five dollars. Quickly slipping the money to the poor woman, he told her happily:

"See what God has sent you!"

That's how he was, a small, quiet, plain-looking man. Some called him homely. Everything about him seemed so ordinary. He never stood out in any crowd. A lady of many years summed it up very well:

"Oh, to see that humble little creature you would never think he was a bishop!"

He never asked for anything for himself. If breakfast was not on the table when he came in he would go without it, never thinking to ring the bell for the housekeeper.

He had always slept very little. Now rumors kept going around that he never used his bed at all. Quite a few people who lived and traveled with him at different times said they never could remember seeing him sleeping on a bed, but often saw him stretched out on the floor.

A priest, Father Bach, came to call and found the Bishop fully dressed lying on the floor.

"Are you ill? You should be in bed."

"Oh, I'm all right here," replied Neumann. He looked like a sick man. Father Bach decided this time he must be firm.

"Come, you must go to bed. It's not your choice. You are bishop and you owe it to your diocese to take care of yourself."

Unwillingly, the Bishop obeyed. Father Bach fixed him a warm drink.

"Wine soup," he explained. "Take it and you'll feel better."

Everyone knew Bishop Neumann never drank wine. He took a sip from the cup and put it down.

"That's not soup, Father. It's wine."

"No it's not. Here, have another sip."

Clearly against his own will, the patient finished the drink. Next day he was up again feeling much better. Jokingly he told Father Bach:

"You know, I was wrong. That soup you gave me was good after all!"

No matter how he spent the night—praying, working, sleeping on the bare floor or out on a sick-call—he was always up before five o'clock. During missions and other special events he would be opening the church doors as early as four. He would light the lamps, prepare the altars, even clean the floor. He made sure everything was in order for the services. He could easily have been mistaken for the sexton.

Following the example of Alphonsus Liguori, he had taken a vow never to waste a moment of time. This too was part of the hidden life. And one day each month he spent in retreat at the Redemptorist house.

He had wanted for some time to introduce the Forty Hours in his diocese. This devotion was centuries old. It consisted of forty hours of continuous prayer, with the Blessed Sacrament exposed on the altar and many candles shedding their soft glow over the people who came to pray and watch by turns—all day, all night. He had dreamed of having this wonderful act of prayer in his own city, first in one church, then another, in a continuous chain of silence and sacrifice throughout the year.

His priests, however, opposed the idea. They remembered days not too long before when churches in Philadelphia had been broken into and burned by rioting mobs. Bitter feelings still existed, hidden perhaps, not as open but nevertheless as real. Wouldn't it be risking serious trouble, they asked, to expose the Blessed Sacrament during the night?

There was truth in what they said. Still, the idea would not leave him. What should he do?

One night very late as he puzzled over this question, alone at his writing desk, tiredness overcame him. His head dropped on the desk and his eyes closed. He didn't mean to sleep, but . . . suddenly he was jerked awake by the sharp smell of something burning. He jumped up in alarm. The candle by whose light he had been working, writing out a plan for the Forty Hours Devotion, had burned down, setting fire to the papers. All were charred and burned. Only the words he had written about the Forty Hours were not touched.

It was, for him, a sign to go ahead.

EIGHT

The Gentle Bishop

It was Neumann's friend, Archbishop Kenrick, who had first called him "The Gentle Bishop."

Writing to the Allen family when Neumann first went to Philadelphia, Kenrick had said:

"You will all love him as your spiritual father; he is so full of kindness and holy. . . . I shall commend you to his kind care, and he will be a guide to you in the ways of holiness."

But it was not only in Philadelphia that guides in the ways of holiness were needed.

If that was a "modern" city in the 1850's, the rest of the diocese was still largely wilderness.

Here in the back country, with its steep mountains and valleys cut through by many rivers, most of the German-speaking people settled. There were towns growing up too. . . .

McKeesport, rising in curves and terraces from the banks of the Monongahela; Sharpsburg, grimy industrial town squeezed in between the Allegheny River and sheer limestone cliffs; Sligo, with one of the first blast furnaces, and pink and white dogwood in springtime offsetting the smoke and smudge; Pottsville, a rugged steep-hilled mountain boom town; Mauch Chunk, a cramped gorge where the first coal was actually mined commercially in America.

Men were just beginning to realize that whole towns were underlaid with solid coal. They knew it only when the main streets of towns began to buckle and shift and telltale smoke rising from the ground far from mine-shafts told of underground fires burning endlessly deep in the earth. Mining as an industry had begun very slowly because people were not used to coal and did not know how valuable it could be.

Indians had planted the first corn in Pennsylvania, cultivating it with hoes made of sharpened stone or the shoulder blade of a moose. Now the foreign-born were flocking to these same fields, farmers and unskilled workers for whom the cities held few opportunities to make a living.

Everywhere one went, Penn's colony told stories of America's past. In Bucks County was the spot, now marked by a bridge, where Washington crossed the Delaware and where there seemed to linger visions of tired Continental soldiers making their slow and silent way across the ice-choked river to surprise the enemy on the Jersey shore. And there was Valley Forge, "darkest winter in American history."

Out there scattered through the wild countryside and crude towns were priests, brave solitary men of God whose labors and hardships can never be told. Neumann had gone through it all in North Bush. That was why he was out very often visiting them, spending six or seven weeks at a time traveling from outpost to outpost, never missing one and never slighting them with hasty and brief "official" calls. As bishop it was his job to make the rounds of his diocese at respectable intervals to administer confirmation and inspect the records and conditions of each parish. As John Neumann it was his dearest responsibility to spend time working with his missionaries.

Railroads were being built, and though many were one-track, these steel roads helped him get around his vast territory. Roads were improving too, and stages bumped over them at fairly regular intervals. It took three days to go that way from Philadelphia to Pittsburgh, at the rate of two cents a mile for each passenger!

Still, traveling conditions in most places were primitive. The Bishop had to cross rivers that had no bridges and climb on foot the sheer faces of mountains where no horse could go. The prophet Isaiah had written: "How beautiful upon the mountains are the feet of him that bringeth good tidings. . . ." (Is. lii, 7)

What did he mean? In reality the feet of the missionary were usually muddy, blistered, frost-bitten, achingly weary. Yet they bore the word of God, the Sacraments of life and death; they bore saints whose names we may never hear, who carried their holy faith across the land.

In the hill town of Bellefonte Neumann could hardly recognize the man who met him. Father Kopf did not look like a priest at all in his battered hat and workman's trousers. He didn't even have a carriage, but for this occasion he had managed to borrow one. After all, bishops did not come to call every day. The horses, frightened by the shrill train whistle and hissing steam, began to bolt. Poor Father Kopf had all he could do to hold them from running away. It was not just the welcome a visiting prelate might expect, but the keen eyes of this visitor had taken in the whole situation the moment he stepped off the train.

"Father Kopf," he said, after greeting his disheveled host, "instead of going back to your mission right away, I wonder if we might stop in town a little while. There are a few things I must buy."

The "few things" turned out to be a good suit of clothes for Father Kopf, who once again began to look and feel like the pastor he was. Then they started for Bellefonte, a hard drive over the Seven Mountains. At the little village of Pottersban they left the horses to continue on foot over the mountains. They met some country people who could offer them only homemade whiskey —"mountain dew," as they called it. In spite of their thirst they refused it.

After confirmation ceremonies in Bellefonte they set out for Lock Haven twenty-five miles away. On a covered bridge a four-horse wagon smashed into them, splintering their wagon-tree. They had to tie the horses behind the wagon and pull it along themselves until they came to a place where some rope could be found to make repairs. As Lock Haven came into view, Father Kopf tried to shorten the journey by pulling harder and harder. Bishop Neumann for once had to protest: "If we break down again, I won't pull any more."

It was important that all Catholics should receive the Sacraments, no matter how far they lived from any church or road. Bishop Neumann made many trips lasting a whole day or more just so that one of these isolated souls would not be deprived.

"Are there any others in your parish still not confirmed?" he asked Father Kopf one evening as they returned from another exhausting day of travel.

"Well—" the good Benedictine hesitated, knowing very well what the Bishop would want to do. "There is one boy—but he's too far away."

"Where does he live?" inquired the Bishop.

"Over at Snow Shoe. The only road there is steep and rough. It's too much of a trip to make for just one child."

The expected answer was not long in coming, in the Bishop's usual gentle voice: "Hasn't that one boy a soul to be saved?"

Father Kopf knew how it would turn out. Mentally, he was already drawing on his heaviest boots and making ready for the twenty-five-mile walk. They started early next morning. Not until nightfall did they come within sight of the Black Moshannon's horseshoe curve, believed by the Indians to be a hoofprint of the great steed of Chattamicco, a mythical hero.

Father Kopf remarked on that trip later:

"The only bed in the house was given to the Bishop, which, however, he did not touch, whilst I with the rest of the family roosted on the hay-mow!"

Another time a priest asked Neumann to wait at the railroad station, explaining apologetically that he had to try to borrow a vehicle to take them to their destination. The Bishop waited patiently until at last the priest returned with a horse hitched to a manure wagon. A single plank laid across the wagon provided the only "seat." It was the best he could do. Without a word the Bishop proceeded to tie his baggage securely to the plank and then climb aboard. The wagon was so low that even a short man found it hard to keep his feet from dragging on the ground. It was raining hard and mud spattered them from head to foot.

Here, as so often on similar occasions, Neumann's sense of humor came to the rescue. He pictured to himself a European bishop traveling in his customary fine carriage. What a shock he would get to see how American dignitaries got around, perched on a slivery plank over a farm wagon!

Eventually they had to pause before a crude blockhouse in the forest. The poor people who lived there welcomed them with sincere good will. They all huddled before the open fireplace trying to keep warm. The unexpected visitors were treated with the greatest respect in the midst of their lowly surroundings. Clothes and baggage were carefully set to dry by the fire, and the one bed was made ready for the Bishop while his companion was given the hayloft. The Bishop, who did not mind at all the inconvenience of the accommodations, was greatly moved by the simple generosity of these farmers. In fact, it was something he met constantly in his travels and which had led him to prefer the rough hospitality of a mountain log cabin to the somewhat strained politeness of a Philadelphia mansion.

With country people he was always good-humored and sociable. He thoroughly enjoyed these evenings around a blazing fire or a rough-hewn table. Some of the stiffer citizens of Philadelphia would have been surprised to see how different he was in places where he felt truly welcome and at home.

A wealthy lady once invited him to a banquet and came to take him to her home after confirmation on one of his journeys. He quietly explained to her that he could not leave the house where he was without hurting the people's feelings. How would they feel if he left a poor home to visit a rich one?

As the years of John Neumann's reign as Philadelphia's bishop stretched on, churches sprang up everywhere. It was like a litany, the names of saints showering down like a rain of grace. This building of churches went on at an almost furious speed. It was unbelievable, especially as he had no money at all to spend on them. No money, and many debts! Like a thread winding through the Pennsylvania countryside, like a thread winding through John Neumann's later years were these churches. With them came the schools, and the priests, brothers and nuns. Orphanages followed, and hospitals and colleges. A seminary was started, for Neumann was one of the first to realize that if the Church in America were to prosper she must produce her own priests instead of depending upon missionaries from other lands. He opened the first school for Negro children in Philadelphia.

In the city itself the litany started: St. Teresa; St. Magdalen of Pazzi, the first church for Italians in the diocese; St. Alphonsus, for of course the holy patron had to be named; Our Lady of Sorrows; St. Bridget and St. Malachy, for there were many Irish Catholics, too. Twenty churches were built and paid for during the summer of 1853 alone!

Then the thread wound out through the mountains, through the towns in the tight valleys, past log cabins perched precariously on cliffs: St. Mary's in Salem, N.J.; St. Joseph's in Dallastown, Pa.; St. Boniface's in St. Clair; St. Francis' in Trenton; St. Peter's in Progress, N.J.

In Patterson there was St. Bartholomew's; in Ivy Mills, St. Thomas'; in Drumore, St. Catherine's; and at Blossburg, St. Andrew's. In Troy was the church named for Neumann's own saint, John Nepomucene.

This was to continue throughout his life, a never-ending work. Some were little chapels, some more elaborate, but all were built "on a shoestring." St. Gregory's in Philadelphia itself (now Our Lady of Sorrows) started out as little more than a tool shed and grew into a great city parish.

Of course, John Neumann himself would have been the last to take credit for this amazing achievement. He would have said it was all due to the good hard-working priests and the generous faithful. To be sure, it was! Yet none of it would have been done without the inspiration, advice, encouragement and bold action of the man in the house on Logan Square. To him the bills came, and he worried night after night over how they would be paid.

Yet it is a strange fact that the man responsible for all of this great work thought himself a failure, unworthy of his office. He often spoke of being unable to handle business matters. When people criticized him for being "impractical" or a poor manager, he agreed completely.

At home, when he was at home, the Bishop often prayed through the night. If anyone rang the doorbell during the very late hours, he would answer it himself. An emergency sick-call? He was already off and on his way, without waking his assistant priests or even letting them know he was going. Sometimes he would arrive home again just in time for early morning Mass. No one ever knew whether he had had any rest or not, and if he was tired one couldn't tell, for he seemed to be always exactly the same.

In the summer of 1853 a violent wave of anti-Catholic feeling swept over the country. Certain groups focused their fear and resentment on the Church. In the midst of this sad time, Bishop Neumann had become involved in a sordid court case over the ownership of one of the churches in Philadelphia. His opponents were Catholic laymen who wished to control all Church property themselves. The case dragged on. The newspapers were filled with humiliating and insulting references to the Bishop.

At the height of the controversy, a visitor from Rome, Archbishop Gaetano Bedini, appeared. Bedini was nuncio to the court of Emperor Pedro II of Brazil, but he came to America on a special mission for the Pope. The Holy Father had heard so many reports about attacks on the Church, particularly the trial involving Bishop Neumann, that he wished his representative to investigate the matter personally. The Italian prelate, accustomed to the pomp and ceremony of Rome, had to face a severe shock as he traveled the still rutted and muddy roads of America.

Bishops in muddy boots? Priests wearing overalls and riding crude farm wagons? In Europe one never saw such things. Surely it was highly unsuitable for churchmen to live like this. The Archbishop's visit to Philadelphia did nothing to soothe his ruffled feelings. The city was unquestionably taking the lead in art, culture and commerce. Social life was thriving. But the Bishop! Neumann was a most unconventional bishop, with his frayed collar, much-mended sleeves, and heavy shoes that had weathered so many storms.

The presence of Bedini in America gave the enemies of the Church a good chance to press their attacks. He was clearly an unwelcome visitor. Riots broke out and in several places he was hanged in effigy.

Bishop Neumann wisely avoided any public welcoming demonstration, fearing it would provoke disorder and physical harm to the Roman official. Bedini's brief stay in Philadelphia gave him a rather one-sided view of the diocese, for he had no time to visit the rural areas where so much of Neumann's work was being done.

As might be expected, Bedini's report to Rome was not altogether favorable. Although he found the American Church as a whole coming along admirably, he had some reservations about the Bishop of Philadelphia. He took special exception to Neumann's short stature. A bishop, Bedini believed, ought to look much more commanding. Here is part of his report:

> The Bishop of Philadelphia seems a little inferior for the importance of such a distinguished city, not in learning nor in zeal nor in piety, but because of the littleness of his person and his neglect of the fashions. . . . He is not able to forget the very humble customs of the Order to which he belongs, but the populous City of Philadelphia, rich, intelligent, full of life and importance, surely merits a bishop of another type.

Neumann himself was sadly aware that he had not made a good impression on his distinguished guest. Later he sent Kenrick a letter of apology for the whole mix-up, taking full blame for all that went wrong:

> On the first arrival of Msgr. Bedini things did not go on as they should, partly on account of my having to leave for the visitation, partly for the

shortness of time . . . but above all for the fact of my being the poorest hand in creation for arranging celebrations or ceremonies. . . . With the best will to do things like others, and to make myself amiable, I make every time more blunders and say more nonsense. . . . I have had this disposition all my life and all the pains my mother, my professors, friends and brothers have ever taken with me were fruitless and thrown away. I will have to keep it with all its consequences until God Almighty will make an end. Would to God that the last act of mine may not be an everlasting misstep!

NINE

Through an Ancient Gate

In the city of Rome, Pope Pius IX gathered together some six hundred letters from Catholic bishops everywhere. They had answered an important question. For a long time people had been begging the Holy Father to speak out in his capacity as Vicar of Christ and proclaim to the world that Mary the Mother of Jesus was "immaculately conceived"—that is, without the slightest sin from the first moment of her life. Finally Pius IX had asked the bishops whether he should take this step. Almost all said yes.

Now he had set the date for the historic proclamation: December 8, 1854. The pontiff whose reign was marked by exile and many other trials was himself sustained by his great devotion to the Mother of God. He looked upon this event as the high point of a difficult life. The revealed word of God, underlined by Mary's message to Catherine Labouré, would be announced to all the world as a truth of the Faith. A huge celebration was planned and invitations had been sent bidding all bishops come to Rome to take part.

Out in the Atlantic, the steamship *Union* tossed in heavy seas. She was ten days out of New York and loaded with as frightened and seasick a crowd of passengers as could be found. Holding the ship's rail firmly with one hand, Bishop Neumann tried to focus his eyes on the blurry pages of a black book held in the other.

He was going to Rome, to the Eternal City, at the Pope's invitation, to attend the great ceremony.

He raised his eyes and looked out over the dark wet peaks rising endlessly. In the splashing mist he saw . . . himself, some eighteen years before, going along this same dangerous route in the other direction. That young man had had no money, no friends, not even the sacred though invisible sign of the priesthood.

Now, with amazement and unbelief, he found himself returning to Europe as the bishop of an important large diocese. The frantic motion of the ship made everything whirl and spin. The *Union* was fighting for survival in that "Black Year" of terrible ocean storms. Neumann had left New York harbor on October 21st, and in ten days more, if the Good Lord protected them, they would dock at Le Havre. Then it would be on to Rome, and after that to Bohemia, his boyhood home!

The feverish activity of the crew only added to the passengers' alarm. At any moment the *Union* might give way, crack up under the battering of so many tons of water, sink to the bottom, bringing all on board. . . . John Neumann caught himself up and brought his scattered thoughts to order hurriedly.

It was all in the Blessed Mother's hand. She was the reason for the journey. She would see to their safety. Thrusting the damp book into a damper pocket, he made his way crookedly across the lurching deck. At least on this trip he had a room to himself, and there he could pray as long as he wished without interruption or ridicule.

Through the vast Basilica of St. Peter the glorious tones of the hymn rang out triumphantly:

"Come, Holy Ghost—"

The Pope, taller and more imposing than ever in his rich robes and jewelled triple crown, rose. A great silence fell over the crowd. He began:

> We declare, pronounce, and define that the doctrine which holds that the most Blessed Virgin Mary was, in the first instant of her conception, by a singular grace and privilege of Almighty God, in virtue of the merits of Christ Jesus, the Saviour of the human race, preserved free from all stain of original sin, is revealed by God, and on that account is to be firmly and constantly believed by the faithful.

Those close enough saw tears on the Holy Father's face as he finished.

Thus the solemn and stirring words were spoken before the huge gathering of the faithful from many lands. Neumann was among them, speechless with wonder. It was a splendid and colorful event, the brilliant vestments of the churchmen reflecting the brilliant gold sunlight streaming into the huge basilica.

For the rest of the day and night it was carnival in Rome. Blazing torches were lighted around St. Peter's, outlining its noble form against the dark sky. Everyone turned out to help celebrate.

Rome's ancient buildings and landmarks, draped with bright bunting, glowed in the light of many candles. In the Piazza di Spagna, the Pope had ordered a tall column erected to mark the event, on top of which was a statue of Our Lady. Her picture was everywhere, large or small, elaborate and simple.

Back in his plain room at the Redemptorist house, Neumann tried to put the happenings of that day into words so his people in Philadelphia could share it with him.

He could only write, at the end: "Thank God I was in Rome for this day!"

A week or so later the rain was pouring over a chillier and much less romantic Rome when the porter of the Redemptorists opened the door to a man in a dripping wet habit of their Congregation.

"Your Excellency! Surely you haven't been out in all this downpour!" said Brother Porter in surprise.

The man smiled. "I wanted to make the pilgrimage of the seven churches today."

The porter spoke before he realized what he was saying: "You've already made it several times, Your Lordship, since your arrival."

Neumann lifted a hand in protest, gentle but firm.

"Please, Brother, it's just 'Father' Neumann here. I'm one of you, remember?" He did not want any special attention among his own religious brothers.

"Excuse me, Father, but your boots are very wet. Did you go on foot all the way? You could have taken the carriage." Clearly the poor Brother did not know his guest very well.

"If you could see some of the roads I've traveled, Brother, in my mission country of Pennsylvania, you wouldn't take any notice of this."

"Then let me ask the Brother in the kitchen to prepare a warm drink for you, to ward off chills."

"Please don't trouble him. I'm quite used to it. I'll just go to my room until supper. I have some letters to write, and I must finish preparing my report for the Holy Father."

What the good Brother did not know was that "Father" Neumann had not eaten anything at all that day. He believed that pilgrimages should be made fasting.

The Holy Father stretched out his hands in greeting to John Neumann, whom he was receiving in private audience. "Here you are, the Redemptorist who didn't want to be a bishop! Tell me now—isn't obedience better than sacrifice?"

The warm smile on the handsome face of the Pope showed that his unusual greeting expressed only affection for the visitor. Pius IX himself had known some very hard times since his election to the Chair of Peter. He had been trapped between temporal and spiritual powers, between those who wanted to rule Italy and those who wanted to rule the Church. He had even been forced by his enemies to flee the Vatican in disguise at night and take refuge in a safer place. His own secretary had been killed, standing beside him, when a bullet from an angry street mob had crashed through the window of the Pope's room.

His fatherly manner quickly put Neumann at ease. Carefully the Bishop of Philadelphia gave his report of affairs in his diocese. The Pope listened closely, clearly satisfied with what he heard.

"But, Your Holiness, there is one problem—"

The Pontiff leaned forward a bit in his heavy chair.

"What is needed most in Philadelphia just now is a home for orphans. I could find a house for them, but I need Sisters to care for them."

"Perhaps the answer is to train them yourself, under the patronage of St. Francis of Assisi," the Pope replied.

Neumann answered slowly. "It does happen

that three women have asked me to allow them to form a religious community. They may be the very ones for our homeless children."

"I advise you then not to delay. Go to the Franciscan Fathers while you are here in Rome," counseled the Pontiff. "They can give you permission to receive these good people into the Third Order of St. Francis."

That is how Neumann became the founder of the Franciscan Sisters of Philadelphia, whose first rule was written in his own precise handwriting.

The business part of the trip over, Neumann could turn to more personal interests. Chief among these was a visit to his Prachatitz home. Slipping off his massive episcopal ring and putting his bishop's cross into his pocket, he set out like an ordinary traveler. First he visited the famous shrine of Loreto and had a look at Venice's canals. Crossing the Italian border into Austria, a gruff guard halted him unceremoniously late one cold night.

"Show your passport! All passengers crossing the border must be identified."

Neumann handed over his papers. The guard looked at them with a puzzled expression. He did not understand English. "Come with me. You'll have to get clearance from the police."

Europe just then was in the throes of revolution. The air was thick with plots and counterplots. A small man with a marked German accent, dressed as a poor priest and trying to slip into Austria with an American passport, was sure to arouse suspicion.

Neumann saw now that traveling as a bishop in disguise had some drawbacks. In trying to escape attention he had in fact attracted more than had he been crossing Europe trailing pontifical robes with all his insignia of office prominently displayed.

"You say you are Bishop of Philadelphia, U.S.A.?" inquired the police chief. The suspicious-looking stranger searched his pockets, finally drawing out a large cross and a ring with its unmistakable episcopal seal. Then he stomped back through piles of snow to continue his journey.

Getting on and off trains and carriages at all hours, it was not surprising he should have lost some of his baggage. The missing package was the one he valued most of all. It held the precious relics he had brought from Rome and the other shrines he had visited along the way.

Dismayed, he stopped at a railroad station and telegraphed back to each place he had stopped. All answers came through the same: Not here . . . not here. Saddened at his loss, he appealed to St. Anthony, promising to hold special devotions to that Keeper of the Heavenly Lost and Found Department if only his precious parcel could be found. It seemed hopeless. How was one small parcel to be traced through Europe?

He had to accept its loss. Saddened, he hardly heard the words of the stranger who suddenly came up to him in the depot.

"Bishop Neumann, here's the package you lost."

The young man thrust the bundle into its owner's hands. Neumann turned in surprise to thank his benefactor. The young man was nowhere to be seen. It was almost as if he had disappeared into the very air. Even more mysteriously, how could anyone in this place have recognized the Bishop of Philadelphia, whose outward appearance gave no hint of his official rank? John Neumann never found out, but soon afterward special prayers to St. Anthony were begun in Philadelphia.

Padua, St. Anthony's hometown, is close to Venice. Had he lost the precious relics there? Certainly he was passing through the great saint's territory!

At Graz, in Austria, he met his boyhood friend and schoolmate, Adalbert Schmidt, now spiritual director of a seminary. Father Schmidt's hopes to join Neumann in America had never been realized.

They had a wonderful visit far into the night.

"Remember, John, that day you were leaving Budweis and I rode with you part of the way in the stagecoach? How sad we both felt at that parting—"

"I'll never forget it. I often think of those long walks we used to take together talking about our future. Now that future is here. We can both be thankful to God for the work He gave us to do, you here in Graz and I in America."

"Yes, you're right. But, tell me, do you ever play the guitar these days?"

Both men laughed at the thought of the Bishop of Philadelphia merrily strumming away an old Bohemian melody in the quiet of his study in staid Logan Square!

He stopped in Prague to see his sister Joan, now Mother Caroline, superior of the Sisters of St. Charles Borromeo. While Bishop Neumann was there, the ex-Emperor Ferdinand invited him to dinner at the castle. How often in his student days he had passed these immense gates, their grilled portals guarded by fierce-looking stone giants armed with clubs and swords! But the man who lived now amid all these splendors was a ruler no longer.

Emperor Ferdinand and his Minister, Prince

Metternich, had been fortunate to escape alive during the 1848 revolution. Now the imperial crown was worn, none too happily, by Ferdinand's nephew, Franz Josef, in Vienna. Neumann's former advisor, Father Dichtl, was Ferdinand's confessor and spiritual support. During the meal, the former ruler conferred upon Neumann membership in an honorary society and also gave him, on a silver platter, a large amount of money in gold United States coins to help in building the Philadelphia cathedral. Soon afterward, Neumann was on the road to Budweis.

There he visited his old school, the Budweis Gymnasium, and the seminary where he had first decided to become a missionary so long ago. But he was impatient to be off. Prachatitz was very near and he felt drawn toward home.

He had hoped to slip into town quietly during the night, but in Prachatitz everyone already knew he was coming. The town fathers had agreed upon a magnificent all-out welcome for this local boy who had made good in a very special way. Plans were made and nothing was forgotten, not even John Neumann's well-known dislike for the limelight!

Adalbert Benesch, a Prachatitz boy going to school in Budweis, had been posted as a spy and courier. When he learned just when Neumann planned to start for his hometown, Adalbert set out along the road on foot. From house to house he went giving the news all the way back to Prachatitz. A feverish excitement ruled beneath the snow-covered roofs. Flags and bunting went up overnight, and in the music-hall trumpeters and drummers and singers practiced for their greatest performance.

That's how it happened that Neumann, gliding squeakily over the hard-packed snow in a rather ramshackle sleigh, found a great surprise awaiting him. All along the "Golden Way" he saw large numbers of people out, kneeling in the snow by the roadside asking for his blessing. He wondered how it happened they were out so early on this cold winter morning.

Outside of Prachatitz they halted.

"I'll walk the rest of the way," he told the driver. "I know all the back roads."

Years ago, he had slipped away from them in such fashion. Then it hadn't mattered so much, but this time it was a matter of civic pride. One of the local members of the nobility, Prince Schwartzenburg, had sent his own splendid sleigh with four handsome horses and a coachman in bright livery to escort the Bishop home. Nothing would do but he must climb into it and drive off with all the bells in the area ringing a welcome. From lookout posts along the hilltops where for centuries guards had watched over the Bohemian Forest to warn the people of any approaching danger, guns boomed out, not in warning this time. It was bitter cold, but no one seemed to feel it. The band struck up its loudest tune, and triumphal sounds filled the thin, biting morning air. Now they passed under the town gate decked with pine boughs newly cut.

John Neumann had never sought popular acclaim and popular acclaim had never sought him. Yet that day he must have felt very happy in the midst of that sincere outpouring of affection from his own people. He could hardly help seeing how heartfelt it was, and he must have been touched in spite of himself.

First he visited St. James's Church. After that he made his way through the crowded street, shaking hands, blessing and speaking to people all the time, up the small hill to his own house.

There in the doorway stood his father, stooped and frail under the burden of his more than eighty years. John's sister Louise was waiting too. The old man looked a bit puzzled. Such a commotion! John a bishop? Yes, that's what they had told him, over and over. That's what John's letters said. But he still couldn't quite believe it. Philadelphia seemed very far away, very unreal. Much easier it was for Philip Neumann to remember his son as a little boy running through the fields, or curled up in a corner with his book.

That week at home was wonderful! At the end of it, he managed to have his own way at last. John Neumann stole away from there in the early morning, before daybreak, with no good-bys, just as he had before. No one knew of his plan except one priest who went with him. At the town gate, one last look back. The figure of old Rozmberk, he of the prancing steed, seemed to be wavering a bit on his horse and the words of his bold motto seemed to run together as in melting ice, or tears. Only a moment, then on the way again!

The house on Logan Square was "home" for him now. After twenty-three wonderful weeks, he must hurry back there. His people, his work awaited him.

On the way he stopped to visit some friends in Munich, Germany. He went out for a walk and there his own personal raincloud caught up with him again. It was a terrible downpour!

"You'd better change those wet shoes before dinner," his host advised.

"If I do," the Bishop answered, "I'll have to put the right one on the left foot, for I have only this pair!"

So he returned, reaching Philadelphia on his birthday, March 28th. He had seen the glories of Rome, the shrines and holy places of Europe and had known the blessed joys of reunion and homecoming. Still, he had but one pair of shoes, and over his head a storm was brewing that would make all the others till now seem like mere sun-showers!

TEN

The Storm Cloud Breaks

When he was made Bishop of Philadelphia, Neumann had chosen a motto: "Passion of Christ, comfort me!" On his official coat of arms these words appeared beneath the Cross. There too was the stalk of hyssop and the lance.

The bitter year of 1856, scarred with tragedy and the sickening sense of being unwanted, proved he had chosen well.

On July 17th St. Michael's Parish was to hold its annual outing at Fort Washington, about fourteen miles from Philadelphia. Everyone looked forward to a wonderful day. A special ten-car train was to carry the picnickers to the country, leaving at six in the morning.

Seven hundred children, their parents and their priest, Father Sheridan, began arriving at the railroad station early that bright summer day. All were in a holiday mood. As usual, there were some stragglers. Greeting one another gaily, shifting their bundles of picnic fare, they didn't notice the time for departure was so near.

"'Board! All aboard!"

Vainly the conductor urged them to take their places quickly so the train could pull out. He knew they must leave right on time in order to reach a safe siding outside the city before the next train was due in from the other direction. Only one track led in and out of Philadelphia. A few seconds made quite a difference.

Still some lagged behind. The smaller children had to be hauled by the hand up the steps. Finally the doors were closed. It was ten minutes after six when the starting signal reached the engineer in his cab up ahead. He checked his big watch. If he gave the engine full steam he would make it to the safety of the siding just in time. Firing up to highest speed, he sent the train careening wildly out of the station and roaring through Philadelphia. In the coaches there was only the pleasant hubbub of happy chatter; in the cab, mounting fear.

Only ten minutes late! Ten minutes that could never be made up—for now the incoming train, right on schedule, rushed toward them. Neither had time to stop. Like fierce animals in combat, the two engines rushed at one another, snorting and spouting fire and smoke. They crashed with a terrible sound of crushing steel. Searing death was upon the passengers before they knew what had happened.

The rest was screams of agony, wreckage and bodies strewn about, desperate efforts to rescue those for whom there was still hope.

When there was time to count, sixty-five were dead, including Father Sheridan, and hundreds more injured.

Bishop Neumann was on a missionary tour when the news came. His school! His children! Horrified, he rushed back. From hospital to hospital he searched until he had found them all. He gave them the Sacraments. He sat beside them hour after hour trying to find words of consolation and encouragement.

But the shock he tried so bravely to wipe away from their minds haunted his own. Over and over he seemed to hear that sickening shudder of steel on steel. Even in the quiet hours of darkness, when everyone else slept, the ghostly vision did not leave him. Resolutely he prayed, turning his thoughts to God, Whose mysterious will, he knew, had somehow been done among those shattered bodies. He labored at his usual tasks with doubled effort. Nothing helped.

No one knew how much he suffered. He never could tell others his deepest thoughts. While he endured the long ordeal, he appeared to be his usual unemotional self. And some, with blind spirits, even called him cold! They didn't know that men like him live only to give others comfort, never to ask it for themselves.

Afterward, his kindness to children was even greater than before—in memory perhaps of those he would never bless again.

This year he could have no peace of mind. He knew he was unwanted, that Philadelphia did not like him as its bishop. Some said he was too short and shabby. Others complained about his foreign accent. Businessmen said he was a bad manager, spending too much money on churches and schools, piling up heavy debts he couldn't pay off. German-speaking groups turned against him because he did not favor them above all others. Many had felt all along that he should never have been appointed bishop.

To understand this shocking state of affairs, we must remember that there was a very strong anti-Catholic feeling in America at that time. The young nation was suffering growing pains and had not yet learned the difference between patriotism, which makes us love and serve our own country, and nationalism, which makes us hate and fear other countries. The Know-Nothing Movement had strongly brought out this anti-foreign, anti-Catholic feeling. Many looked upon the Catholic pope as a foreign power plotting to seize control of the government in Washington. Priests, as the Pope's representatives, were also held in suspicion. How could these subjects of an Italian ruler be good Americans?

Peace-loving William Penn would not have been proud of his City of Brotherly Love at that time. His charter had carefully stated that freedom of religion must never be denied any man. In the Quaker colony of Penn's Woods many religious groups had found refuge and welcome in their search for liberty. Yet Philadelphia had become one of the most anti-Catholic and intolerant cities in America. Not long before, in Bishop Kenrick's time, rioting mobs had destroyed rectories, burned figures of priests in public squares, and set torches to churches. Though violence had ceased by 1856, it was an uneasy peace. Strong feelings were still there, thinly disguised by a polite exterior.

To be a Catholic priest was enough to make any man unpopular. To be a Catholic bishop with a foreign accent in the bargain was just too much! Americans were already forgetting that their own fathers or grandfathers had come from Europe too, and had come very often in search of the same freedom they now denied to others.

As for the Catholics—to put it bluntly, they were ashamed of their bishop. Philadelphia liked to consider itself a cultural center, as indeed it was to some extent. It had many elegant houses and "society" families. Art, music and literature were flourishing.

Catholics, however, had often been looked down upon as belonging to the "lower" classes. Trying hard to make a good impression, they were embarrassed by Neumann's plain appearance, his insignificant size, his lack of sophistication and polish, his utter disregard of social formalities. They would have liked someone with a bit more style, someone who would appear at all the proper places, wearing the proper clothes, saying all the proper things to the very, very proper upper-class Philadelphians. This, they thought, would prove beyond doubt that Catholics were as good as anyone else. And this, they knew, Bishop Neumann was never going to do!

Even the priests resented this, though, if the truth were known, very few of them could compare with their bishop in learning and wisdom.

Early one Sunday morning Neumann, hurrying briskly to a near-by church, met Father John Bach.

"Bishop, you do look shabby!" exclaimed Father Bach. "Today is Sunday, after all. Please go back and change your coat."

"How can I?" replied the Bishop. "I have no other."

He hadn't. He had given his good coat to a poor man that very morning, only a few minutes before. Except for his bishop's cross and ring, both of which now weighed as heavily upon him as if forged of iron, there was nothing distinctive in the way he looked. His hats were always old, tinged with green, showing the effects of many rainstorms. His shoes, certainly not chosen for looks, might have been more suitable for climbing in the Böhmerwald than for walking Philadelphia's neat brick walks and tidy grass-bordered paths. As a fashion-plate he was a total failure, though he always shined his shoes and brushed his clothes so that they were neat and clean.

"But you must realize," Father Bach went on, "that you aren't just a missionary bishop. This is Philadelphia! You're not on the prairies with the Indians!" The priest turned and his arm, encased in a well-tailored sleeve, made a sweep of the city around them. "This is a *very* civilized city. What if you were to appear at the new Academy of Music looking like that?"

Harsh words, insulting words, bold disrespectful words! It wasn't the first time the Bishop had heard them.

Gently he answered, "I'm not going to the Academy of Music, Father. I'm going to church. But I'll tell you something my mother once said to one of my sisters when we were all children in Bohemia. My sister was complaining that her clothes weren't as fashionable as those of her friends, and my mother told her: 'If you hope to impress others merely through fine clothes, you show by that very fact that you are worth nothing at all.'"

Father Bach's face showed his impatience. "But your vestments—even they aren't fit to be worn by a bishop!"

"Don't forget, Father, I'm not only a bishop. I'm a Redemptorist. Our founder, St. Alphonsus Liguori, was a nobleman by birth. He was also a bishop. Yet he wore a ring worth about twenty-five cents, and used the same shoes he had for his consecration for the rest of his life—twenty-five years!"

Although Neumann could converse in twelve languages, his English was never as eloquent and graceful as some would have liked. They went to church on Sunday to hear fine words from the pulpit and were actually offended to have to listen to plain truths plainly spoken—in a German accent.

For those who flocked to Neumann's confessional, hour after weary hour, year after long year, it was a different story. As bishop he did not have to hear confessions. His other duties would have excused him, yet all his life he devoted much of his time to this humble, trying and majestic work. In the darkness of the confessional his short stature and unfashionable attire had no importance. He was merely a presence who understood everything and, in the name of Almighty God, forgave. To many souls who had carried heavy burdens for a long time simply because they could not confess in English, this was heaven-sent.

It is one thing to learn how to ask for a sack of flour in a new language, but when it comes to the secrets of the heart only one's own tongue will do. No one knew this better than Neumann. He even learned Gaelic so he could help new arrivals from Ireland. He must have learned it very well too, for one old Irish lady, coming from confession, exclaimed with wonder and relief: "At last we have an Irish bishop!"

This "Irish" bishop was of course none other than the awkward-speaking Bohemian whose conversation did not meet the standards of high society!

If there was anyone who agreed heartily that the Bishop of Philadelphia was the most unworthy man ever to wear a pectoral cross, it was John Neumann. No one saw his shortcomings, if they were shortcomings, more clearly than he. No one was more eager to do something about them. Twice he had written his resignation and twice had burned it. To resign was not the answer. Deeply troubled, well aware of all that was being said about him, he spent night after night in prayer, trying to see a way out. The American bishops were to gather soon in Baltimore for their Eighth Provincial Council. Here was his chance!

His fellow prelates listened politely as Bishop Neumann began to speak. He told them he felt he couldn't handle such an important post as the Philadelphia diocese, with its 145 churches and nearly 200,000 souls. He proposed that the diocese be divided in two. The new see might be at Pottsville, a rugged, steep-hilled town on the edge of the coal mine region. Until now, the other bishops had followed him with interest. What he said next, though, startled them considerably.

"If this were done, I would be happy to leave

Philadelphia and take the See of Pottsville instead."

Pottsville? Who would want to be bishop there, in that humble corner of nowhere, working among coal miners, poor farmers and struggling immigrants in the Pennsylvania back country?

Neumann gave his answer in a letter to Cardinal Franzoni in Rome:

> The City of Philadelphia . . . needs someone else instead of myself who am too plain and not sufficiently talented. Besides I love solitude. . . . I am most willing to be transferred to another See where a less gifted man would be required. For more than fifteen years I worked on the North American missions. I have loved corporal labors and journeys in the mountains and through the forests. . . .

To another church official, he wrote with deep and moving simplicity:

> I have always loved the labors of a missionary, travels, visitations, the heat of summer and the cold of winter. . . . I despair of ever making any progress in the accomplishments of this world. . . . Visiting Catholic families separated by long distances and preaching to them, etc., has been my greatest joy. . . .

The matter had been referred to Rome, where any decision must be made. In the long winter of

1856 many letters went back and forth between the Vatican and various Church officials in America, arguing the pros and cons of Bishop Neumann's merits and failings. Rumors flew. When the priests and people of Philadelphia heard them, they felt they no longer owed him loyalty or obedience.

One day, at a meeting of priests, Neumann proposed that the people should not be asked to pay money at the church door before Mass because this made the poor stay away.

The others disagreed. One priest rose and gave a sharp, insulting reply. There was an angry, defiant tone in his voice that showed all too clearly how little he respected his bishop. It was a painful and personal attack. In the silence that followed, Neumann spoke as calmly as ever:

"Since you seem to disagree with me, and I have good reason for my opinion, let's put the question before the Holy See for a decision."

Something in this answer brought instant remorse to all present. Was it humility? Was it superhuman self-control? The attacker put it clearly as he went out from the meeting, ashamed:

"We have a holy Bishop."

That was the strangest thing of all about those trying days. Never in any letter or complaint, no matter how bitter, did Neumann's critics fail to assert strongly that he was a holy man.

In fact, the word "holy" stands out on nearly every page of that endless correspondence. No wonder Rome was confused. In the same breath that they declared him holy, the fault-finders declared him unfit to be bishop.

At last Rome acted. Early in 1857 a helper was appointed, an assistant bishop who would share the burdens. The man chosen for the post was James Wood, a native Philadelphian and a convert to Catholicism. He was a brilliant man, a wonderful speaker, tall and commanding in appearance, with a manner that put him at ease everywhere. He had in great supply all the social graces Neumann lacked. Besides, he had been a banker before becoming a priest and would be an excellent financial manager.

With great relief, Neumann welcomed Bishop Wood, putting into his capable hands the business affairs of the diocese. Now he himself felt almost like a free man once more, free to tramp off into the backwoods to visit his beloved children in the log cabins perched on steep mountainsides. Far from the stiff drawing rooms of Philadelphia, he could relax at a crude timber table, tell stories, share the simple food, entertain the little ones, and give and receive the warmth of genuine love. Here he never felt too short, too awkward or like a foreigner. They called him "Father," these country folk, welcoming him to their bare firesides as they would a dear friend. Gladly they gave him their one good bed for the night, even though they knew ahead of time he would choose to lie on the hard floor. Once more he was what he had chosen to be—a missionary.

Preparing a room for Bishop Wood in the house on Logan Square had presented some problems. There was little enough furniture to begin with, yet the newcomer must be made comfortable. The faithful housekeeper had to use all her resources to make the arrangements half-way suitable, but she could not solve the problem of where the new Bishop was to store his clothes.

Neumann was working at his desk when she raised the question. "Please, Bishop, would you buy a new wardrobe for Bishop Wood? He'll need one in which to keep his clothes."

Neumann took out his purse and opened it, turned it inside out. Empty! No chance of any wardrobes from that source! He thought a moment, then said cheerfully:

"I have the answer. Give him mine. It isn't new, of course, but it will do for the time."

"But, Your Excellency," protested the good woman, "what about yourself?"

"Oh, it's just in the way as far as I'm concerned," was the reply. "I don't need one."

It was true. He had nothing to put into it. His "wardrobe," such as it was, was on his back. Anything extra was immediately given to the poor.

"Yes," thought the housekeeper, making her way down the hall, "and he might as well move his bed out too. He hardly ever uses it!"

ELEVEN

The Perfect Disguise

John Neumann had throughout his lifetime a perfect disguise. Some of it God gave him and the rest he was careful to adopt on his own. It served his purposes very well. It suited him perfectly if people saw in him only a small, unsociable, slightly awkward man with a bit of the soil of the Bohemian Forest still sticking to his boots.

No one would expect great deeds from such a shabby, plain, little person. In fairy tales we sometimes find a hero in disguise, but before the end he always changes back into his true self—dashing, handsome and clever. But this is a true story, and John Neumann kept his disguise right to the end.

Yet he did have what was for him almost a moment of triumph. For seven years, in spite of lack of money and other delays, he had been trying to finish the Cathedral of Saints Peter and Paul in Logan Square. Finally the great building, made fun of by many during its construction, was ready to be roofed. The brownstone front with its giant pillars in classic Greek style was finished; the arches of the dome were set. Workmen scrambled over the top of the structure, laying thousands of bricks row by row. Then they set in place the huge copper-colored dome. It was an impressive sight.

Now the great cross could be placed on top. Though there was still much work to be done inside, this cross symbolized completion. It symbolized much more than that. The only banner under which Neumann had ever marched was now to crown his cathedral as though it crowned his life work.

The feast of the Exaltation of the Holy Cross was chosen for the solemn occasion in that September of 1859. Thousands thronged Logan Square to watch the procession of brilliantly robed clergymen entering the cathedral. The cross, eleven feet high and made of strong Florida pine, painted gold, was set in its place.

Did anyone wonder why, at the solemn High Mass that morning, it was the imposing and dignified Bishop Wood who was celebrant, while Neumann, serving as assistant, was lost in the colorful crowd, and a visiting prelate from Virginia delivered the stirring sermon?

It was a gala day for the Catholics of Philadelphia. For Bishop Neumann it was joyous too. When he looked up at the cross shining in the sunlight, he must have remembered that first bleak day he had spent in America, scurrying about the rain-slicked streets of New York looking vainly for a church that did not have a weather-cock on top.

For the country at large, the fall of 1857 was not a very happy time. The long-threatened crisis over slavery was reaching the boiling point. Many had hoped an open break between North and South could be avoided. Now they shook their heads gloomily over the future.

Feeling ran high on both sides of the Mason-Dixon Line, and throughout the North the abolitionists, in speech and printed word, were whipping up violent reactions with their fiery denunciations of the institution of human bondage. In the South, on the other hand, the invention of the cotton gin and the booming growth of the cotton and sugar plantations made slaves seem more necessary than ever.

It was now two years since Chief Justice Taney had handed down the Supreme Court decision in the case of Dred Scott, a slave from Missouri. Scott, taken by his owner into the Louisiana territory where slavery was outlawed by the Missouri compromise, sued for his freedom. The nation's highest court refused his plea, stating that no Negro could ever be a United States citizen and therefore no Negro could bring suit in a United States court. In the South this decision was greeted with delight. It seemed as if the Constitution itself backed slavery. But the matter was far from settled.

When the lanky and little-known politician from Illinois, Abe Lincoln, clambered up on the platform to debate his opponent in the Senatorial race, Stephen A. Douglas, slavery was the main issue. Douglas, the "Little Giant," was tremendously popular. Lincoln was almost unknown. If people had been told that this man would soon be elected President of the United States, they would have refused to believe it.

In the house on Logan Square next to the cathedral, it was business as usual for the Bishop of Philadelphia. He was hard at work. Though years before he had taken a vow never to waste a single minute, now he seemed to redouble his efforts to keep that promise. The clock on the wall was an ever-present reminder to him of the swift passage of time—too swift for one who saw so much to be done! Perhaps there was something besides the clock hurrying him on, some inner timepiece whose faltering beat gave warning of time's end.

People said he was working more strenuously than ever. Churches and schools still a-building must be finished. He urged them steadily forward as if by strength of his will alone the stones, bricks and mortar would fall into their places, the bills for them be paid, the money found to buy more.

The litany of churches continued with surprising speed: St. Mary's in Allentown; St. Patrick's in Canaan; St. Vincent's chapel in Tacony; Holy Cross Church at Union; St. Kieran's in Heckscherville; St. Jerome's, Seven Dolors, and many more in many places.

Unassuming as ever, he still found time for humble duties. On reception-day at the newly formed community of the Sisters of the Good Shepherd, it was always Bishop Neumann who stood at the altar rail to receive the veiled Magdalens and hear their promises of lifelong dedication.

His schedule as always was crowded. On Christmas Eve, at the end of 1859, he heard confessions in his chapel until eleven o'clock. An hour later he presided at the midnight Mass. Afterward he said Mass privately in his chapel and by ten o'clock Christmas morning he was back on the main altar of St. John's for the High Mass.

As the New Year of 1860 came he was full of plans. Momentarily, it was true, he did not feel quite up to all he meant to do. On January 4th he was writing to a nun and saying, just in passing, "I am not feeling well these last few days, otherwise I might have gone up to see Mother Theresa. . . ."

He was sick, certainly, but it wasn't the first time. He paid little attention.

On Thursday, the fifth of January, he seemed especially talkative at the table during the mid-day meal. He entertained Bishop Wood with delightful stories of life in Prachatitz. He told of the farmer who took him aside just before he set off to America and gave him this wise advice:

"Now John, you are going on a long and dangerous voyage. Take my advice. Here are two gold pieces. When you go on board the ship, give these to the captain and tell him he can keep them on condition that he always steers the ship in shallow water near the shore!"

After lunch, the Redemptorist Father Urban stopped for a quick visit. The Bishop looked far from well.

"How do you feel today?" the priest asked, knowing it was a subject that must be tactfully introduced.

The Bishop's eyes, clouded with illness, took on a strange expression, but his voice as usual was calm and clear.

"I have an odd feeling today, Father Urban," he confessed. "I never felt this way before." Then, brushing that topic of conversation aside quickly, he said briskly, "I have to go out on a little business. The fresh air will do me good." Then he added: "A man must always be ready, for death comes when and where God wills."

Father Urban, reassured by Neumann's calm, went away, those last words lying on the top of his mind like an undeciphered code message.

The first errand was a routine matter about property deeds. He had to visit lawyers' offices frequently on such business, much as he disliked that part of his work. Afterward he wanted to go to the express office to inquire about a lost chalice. Father Kopf had sent it to be consecrated, but somehow it had never arrived. As a favor to Father Kopf, Neumann promised to try to track it down or get a new one.

But the express officials did not see him that day. He was on his way there, crossing the street on Vine near Thirteenth Street, when he seemed to stumble. He managed to reach the curb and staggered toward the stoop of the nearest house. Then he fell. The sidewalk was icy. Two men who were passing saw him go down and rushed to help him. They carried him into the house without having any idea who he was. They laid him on a couch. Then the non-Catholic residents of the house happened to notice that he wore a large cross.

Someone ran to the Bishops' house to summon help. Before the priest could hurry over to give the Last Rites, Neumann was dead—without protest or agony, without even a final word.

He had been alone trudging down the cold road to Budweis and across Europe to the sea, and again across the sea, through the streets of New York, and on the canal boat to Rochester and in the dark forests of Niagara country. Neumann was a man who always traveled alone on important journeys.

He was alone that day as he left his house. He was alone a little later as he left the law office. He was alone as he stumbled and fell on the sidewalk. Alone he lay there, and when they carried him into the house he was alone still, for no one knew who he was. The people were not of his faith. Among strangers he died—alone.

Death—shocking, stark, sudden—stripped away the disguise Neumann had worn so well for so long. Now, overnight, grief tore away the "front" and truth broke through.

When Philadelphia heard the news that its bishop was dead, it was the Eve of Epiphany. Priests had already begun reciting the office that tells the story of the Magi bringing their gifts to the Christ Child.

Neumann, too, had brought precious gifts, but because there was nothing kingly in his appearance, because his gifts were so largely to the poor, the needy, the obscure, they had gone unacclaimed. Now those to whom he had given so much came by hundreds to pay homage, moving slowly past his body as it lay in the Cathedral of Saints Peter and Paul. Some still wore clothes he had given them. All remembered some special act of kindness. They wept as they shuffled by. Their lips moved in prayer. They touched their rosaries to the cold body. Things Neumann had held, owned, or blessed were treated as precious relics.

From early morning till late at night they kept coming—laborers, children, gray-haired grandmothers, people of all ages and stations.

The whole city was taken by surprise. Church officials, even some who claimed to have known him well, were completely overwhelmed by the sudden spontaneous public homage. They, too, had been deceived by Neumann's disguise. The news of his holiness, like the news of his death, seemed to strike like lightning. All of his good deeds seemed to rise up to give witness to a remarkable life. In ancient times this outpouring of veneration would have been accepted as proof of saintliness. Only now they learned that he had worn around his waist an iron chain that constantly tore his flesh.

Neumann had had one great desire: to live the simple life of a Redemptorist priest. So he was buried, not in his cathedral where as bishop he rightfully belonged, but in the place he loved—the Redemptorist Church of St. Peter.

It was the largest funeral Philadelphia had ever seen. The muffled drums, the mournful trumpets, the tolling of church bells cast a deep and reverent silence over the crowds that lined the streets, hung over windowsills, even watched from rooftops. As might have been expected, it was raining.

Beyond the sadness there was a strange feeling that some unusual presence had departed. To the crypt of St. Peter's, in flickering candlelight, a unique procession came—the crippled, the deaf, the sick, the poor. They came to pray for Bishop Neumann's help in their tragedies. Some came away cured. Other priests and bishops, awed at first by the outpouring of reverence for their late associate, began to take note of these happenings.

Loveliest of all was the story of the blind child, Mary Hunneker, who was sure the "gentle bishop" would make her see again. Eye doctors had told her there was no hope. She came to pray for nine days at Neumann's tomb. On the ninth day, the darkness went away and she could see.

Newspapers were quick to publicize these stories, but the Church itself waited, cautious as ever in such cases. Years passed. The Cause for the beatification of John Neumann was brought to Rome and investigations dragged on. Those who had known him were no longer living. History books passed over him to praise his successor, the brilliant and impressive Bishop Wood.

At last a meeting was scheduled to decide once and for all whether the fourth Bishop of Philadelphia, again all but forgotten, deserved to be called saintly. It was 1921. Pope Benedict XV would preside. The Cardinals would make the final decision. The priest who served as "Devil's Advocate" was sincerely convinced that they should forget all about John Neumann. He had studied the whole case thoroughly and could not honestly say that he saw anything heroic about Neumann's life. He intended to vote against him, and he had already persuaded many of the Cardinals to do the same.

On his way to the meeting, he stopped for a haircut at a Roman barbershop. The hour of the gathering came. All the others waited, but the priest whose opinion would tip the scales against Neumann had not arrived. Suddenly a messenger hurried in to say that the man they awaited was dead. He had died in the barber's chair not half an hour before.

Some of the Cardinals felt God had shown His will in that strange event. In any case, not one voted no when the question of the heroic virtue of Neumann was decided. If his earthly career seemed lacking in drama, this moment made up for it.

This is being written on October 13, 1963.

The great bells of St. Peter's are pealing for a new "blessed." More than twenty thousand persons have crowded into the great basilica in Rome to hear the formal announcement of the beatification of John Nepomucene Neumann. Pope Paul VI has come to pay homage. Radio and television are broadcasting the story. There is a man kneeling in the vast congregation whose picture has been in newspapers all over the world. He is J. Kent Lenahan, Jr., a Philadelphia musician, whose head and limbs were shattered in an auto accident July 8, 1949, when he was nineteen. His parents had placed a piece of one of

Neumann's worn cassocks on the bed where their son lay close to death. Within hours he had recovered. His cure was one of the official miracles attributed to Blessed John, proved authentic beyond all doubt.

The lights shine brightly, the bells of St. Peter's are ringing triumphantly, and the solemn "Te Deum" is heard through the ancient arches. High above the Altar of the Chair, in the middle of Bernini's magnificent golden "Gloria" window, the "official" portrait of Neumann is unveiled. Here the last of the disguise of the quiet little Bohemian priest is gone. No artist could depict for so solemn an occasion, in so solemn a place, a hero who looked and acted just as the real Neumann had looked and acted. It would not be suitable at all.

The artist therefore made him several inches taller, more imposing, handsomer, more poised and self-possessed than he ever seemed in life. He is wearing brand-new robes, probably much finer than any he ever wore on this earth. The old muddy boots have been replaced by a pair of shiny shoes. He looks at home among the attentive angels that surround him. His pictured presence is suitably infused with that light of glory, that kind of splendor and glow that makes everyone immediately recognize greatness, although no flicker of it ever struck him in real life. At last John Neumann has become, under the artist's brush, the kind of man we demand our heroes to be.

Nowhere in that heavenly mist above his head is there a rain cloud. Not a drop falls to mar his flowing mantle. What would plain John Neumann say if he saw himself standing so, all of his beloved, carefully preserved disguise swept away by a world trying to honor what it can never understand—holiness?

But wait—it's not quite gone. Even today he keeps something of his old blundering self. People looking up from those colorful and impressive ceremonies can see an inscription in large letters on one of the pillars of the basilica. It is a large marble tablet placed there long ago, bearing the names of all the bishops present when the dogma of the Immaculate Conception was defined in 1854. Among the names is that of "Joannes Newman, Episcopus Philadelphiensis."

"Since 1854," someone has remarked, "we have at least learned to spell his name!"

Important Dates in the Life of Bishop Neumann

March 28, 1811	Born at Prachatitz, Bohemia.
November 1, 1823	Entered Budweis Lyceum (High School).
November 1, 1831	Entered seminary at Budweis.
Autumn 1833	Transferred to Prague seminary.
October 1834	Began keeping diary.
July 2, 1835	Left Prague, ready for ordination.
April 20, 1836	Sailed from Le Havre for America.
June 1, 1836	Arrived in New York City.
June 25, 1836	Ordained in Old St. Patrick's Cathedral, New York, by Bishop John Dubois.
June 26, 1836	Celebrated First Mass in St. Nicholas' Church, New York.
July 1836	Began service as missionary priest in upstate New York near Buffalo.
October 1840	Entered Congregation of the Most Holy Redeemer (Redemptorists).
January 16, 1842	Became first Redemptorist to make solemn profession in America.
March 1844	Made Superior of Redemptorists in Pittsburgh, Pa.
March 15, 1847	Appointed General Superior of Redemptorists in America.
1848	Naturalized as American citizen.
March 28, 1852	Consecrated fourth Bishop of Philadelphia by Archbishop Francis P. Kenrick, St. Alphonsus' Church, Baltimore, on 41st birthday.

May 3, 1852	Established pattern of present parochial school system.
Spring 1853	Introduced Forty Hours Devotion on permanent basis first time in United States.
1854	Visited Rome for promulgation of dogma of the Immaculate Conception and stopped at Prachatitz.
April 26, 1857	Coadjutor Bishop James Wood consecrated.
January 5, 1860	Died suddenly on Philadelphia street-corner.
December 11, 1921	Declared Venerable by Pope Benedict XV.
October 13, 1963	Declared Blessed by Pope Paul VI.

VISION BOOKS

All Vision Books have full color jackets, black and white illustrations, sturdy full cloth bindings. Imprimatur.

1. ST. JOHN BOSCO AND THE CHILDREN'S SAINT, DOMINIC SAVIO *by* CATHERINE BEEBE.
2. ST. THERESE AND THE ROSES *by* HELEN WALKER HOMAN.
3. FATHER MARQUETTE AND THE GREAT RIVERS *by* AUGUST DERLETH.
4. ST. FRANCIS OF THE SEVEN SEAS *by* ALBERT J. NEVINS, M.M.
5. BERNADETTE AND THE LADY *by* HERTHA PAULI.
6. ST. ISAAC AND THE INDIANS *by* MILTON LOMASK.
7. FIGHTING FATHER DUFFY *by* VIRGINIA LEE BISHOP *and* JIM BISHOP.
8. ST. PIUS X, THE FARM BOY WHO BECAME POPE *by* WALTER DIETHELM, O.S.B.
9. ST. IGNATIUS AND THE COMPANY OF JESUS *by* AUGUST DERLETH.
10. JOHN CARROLL: BISHOP AND PATRIOT *by* MILTON LOMASK.
11. ST. DOMINIC AND THE ROSARY *by* CATHERINE BEEBE.
12. THE CROSS IN THE WEST *by* MARK BOESCH.
13. MY ESKIMOS: A PRIEST IN THE ARCTIC *by* ROGER BULIARD, O.M.I.
14. CHAMPIONS IN SPORTS AND SPIRIT *by* ED FITZGERALD.
15. FRANCIS AND CLARE, SAINTS OF ASSISI *by* HELEN WALKER HOMAN.
16. CHRISTMAS AND THE SAINTS *by* HERTHA PAULI.
17. EDMUND CAMPION, HERO OF GOD'S UNDERGROUND *by* HAROLD C. GARDINER, S.J.
18. MODERN CRUSADERS *by* JOHN TRAVERS MOORE *and* ROSEMARIAN V. STAUDACHER.
19. OUR LADY CAME TO FATIMA *by* RUTH FOX HUME.
20. THE BIBLE STORY *by* CATHERINE BEEBE.
21. ST. AUGUSTINE AND HIS SEARCH FOR FAITH *by* MILTON LOMASK.
22. ST. JOAN, THE GIRL SOLDIER *by* LOUIS DE WOHL.
23. ST. THOMAS MORE OF LONDON *by* ELIZABETH M. INCE.
24. MOTHER SETON AND THE SISTERS OF CHARITY *by* ALMA POWER-WATERS.
25. ST. THOMAS AQUINAS AND THE PREACHING BEGGARS *by* BRENDAN LARNEN, O.P. *and* MILTON LOMASK.
26. FATHER DAMIEN AND THE BELLS *by* ARTHUR *and* ELIZABETH SHEEHAN.
27. COLUMBUS AND THE NEW WORLD *by* AUGUST DERLETH.
28. ST. PHILIP OF THE JOYOUS HEART *by* FRANCIS X. CONNOLLY.

29. LYDIA LONGLEY, THE FIRST AMERICAN NUN *by* HELEN A. McCARTHY.
30. ST. ANTHONY AND THE CHRIST CHILD *by* HELEN WALKER HOMAN.
31. ST. ELIZABETH'S THREE CROWNS *by* BLANCHE JENNINGS THOMPSON.
32. KATHARINE DREXEL, FRIEND OF THE NEGLECTED *by* ELLEN TARRY.
33. ST. LOUIS AND THE LAST CRUSADE *by* MARGARET ANN HUBBARD.
34. KATERI TEKAKWITHA, MOHAWK MAID *by* EVELYN M. BROWN.
35. ST. BENEDICT, HERO OF THE HILLS *by* MARY FABYAN WINDEATT.
36. THE CURE OF ARS, THE PRIEST WHO OUTTALKED THE DEVIL *by* MILTON LOMASK.
37. CATHOLIC CAMPUSES: Stories of American Catholic Colleges *by* ROSEMARIAN V. STAUDACHER.
38. ST. HELENA AND THE TRUE CROSS *by* LOUIS DE WOHL.
39. GOVERNOR AL SMITH *by* HON. JAMES A. FARLEY *and* JAMES C. G. CONNIFF.
40. KIT CARSON OF THE OLD WEST *by* MARK BOESCH.
41. ROSE HAWTHORNE: THE PILGRIMAGE OF NATHANIEL'S DAUGHTER *by* ARTHUR *and* ELIZABETH ODELL SHEEHAN.
42. THE URSULINES, NUNS OF ADVENTURE *by* HARNETT T. KANE.
43. MOTHER CABRINI, MISSIONARY TO THE WORLD *by* FRANCES PARKINSON KEYES.
44. MORE CHAMPIONS IN SPORTS AND SPIRIT *by* ED FITZGERALD.
45. ST. MARGARET MARY, APOSTLE OF THE SACRED HEART *by* RUTH FOX HUME.
46. WHEN SAINTS WERE YOUNG *by* BLANCHE JENNINGS THOMPSON.
47. FRANCES WARDE AND THE FIRST SISTERS OF MERCY *by* SISTER MARIE CHRISTOPHER, R.S.M.
48. VINCENT DE PAUL, SAINT OF CHARITY *by* MARGARET ANN HUBBARD.
49. FLORENCE NIGHTINGALE'S NUNS *by* EMMELINE GARNETT.
50. POPE PIUS XII, THE WORLD'S SHEPHERD *by* LOUIS DE WOHL.
51. ST. JEROME AND THE BIBLE *by* GEORGE SANDERLIN.
52. SAINTS OF THE BYZANTINE WORLD *by* BLANCHE JENNINGS THOMPSON.
53. CHAPLAINS IN ACTION *by* ROSEMARIAN V. STAUDACHER.
54. ST. CATHERINE LABOURÉ AND THE MIRACULOUS MEDAL *by* ALMA POWER-WATERS.
55. MOTHER BARAT'S VINEYARD *by* MARGARET ANN HUBBARD.
56. CHARLES DE FOUCAULD, ADVENTURER OF THE DESERT *by* EMMELINE GARNETT.

57. MARTIN DE PORRES, SAINT OF THE NEW WORLD *by* Ellen Tarry.
58. MARGUERITE BOURGEOYS, PIONEER TEACHER *by* Sister St. Mary Genevieve, C.N.D.
59. FATHER KINO, PRIEST TO THE PIMAS *by* Ann Nolan Clark.
60. CHILDREN WELCOME: VILLAGES FOR BOYS AND GIRLS *by* Rosemarian V. Staudacher.
61. GREGORY THE GREAT, CONSUL OF GOD *by* George Sanderlin.
62. PETER AND PAUL: THE ROCK AND THE SWORD *by* Blanche Jennings Thompson.
63. IRISH SAINTS *by* Robert T. Reilly.
64. DEAR PHILIPPINE: THE MISSION OF MOTHER DUCHESNE *by* Margaret Ann Hubbard.
65. PETER CLAVER, SAINT AMONG SLAVES *by* Ann Ross.
66. JOHN NEUMANN, THE CHILDREN'S BISHOP *by* Elizabeth Odell Sheehan.